STARGAZING
WITH JACK HORKHEIMER

COSMIC COMICS FOR THE SKY WATCHER

by Jack Horkheimer
with Stephen James O'Meara

Illustrated by Rich Harrington

CRICKET BOOKS

Peterborough, NH

Editorial Director: Lou Waryncia
Editor: Elizabeth Lindstrom
Designer: Maria Reynolds
Proofreader: Eileen Terill

The content of this book first appeared in *ODYSSEY* magazine. The original scripts on which these cartoons are based are from the PBS TV series *Star Gazer*, a production of WPBT Miami, produced in cooperation with the Miami Museum of Science and Space Transit Planetarium.

The Library of Congress Cataloging-in-Publication Data for *Stargazing with Jack Horkheimer* is available at http://catalog.loc.gov.

Cricket Books
a division of Carus Publishing
30 Grove Street
Peterborough, NH 03458
www.cricketmag.com
www.odysseymagazine.com

Printed in China

GREETINGS, GREETINGS, FELLOW STARGAZERS!

EVERY MONTH, **ODYSSEY** MAGAZINE FEATURES "STARGAZING WITH JACK HORKHEIMER," A MONTHLY COMIC STRIP BASED ON MY WEEKLY TELEVISION SERIES ON NAKED-EYE ASTRONOMY CALLED **STAR GAZER**. NOW I'M PLEASED THAT WE'VE JOINED FORCES AGAIN TO CREATE THIS COSMIC COMIC BOOK.

WE ALL LOVE TO LOOK UP IN WONDER AT THE STARS, AND THIS BOOK WILL HELP YOU BETTER UNDERSTAND AND ENJOY WHAT YOU'RE SEEING. IT WILL HELP YOU DISCOVER WONDERS THAT YOU DON'T EVEN KNOW EXIST.

INSIDE, YOU'LL FIND SOME OF THE MOST IMPORTANT STARS AND CONSTELLATIONS, THE PLANETS, AND OTHER GALACTIC OBJECTS THAT ARE VISIBLE TO THE NAKED EYE. YOU'LL ALSO BE INTRODUCED TO BASIC CONCEPTS OF STARGAZING AND TO SOME OF THE MOST MIND-BOGGLING FACTS ABOUT OUR UNIVERSE... ALL PRESENTED FROM THE VIEWPOINT OF A WONDERFUL CAST OF CARTOON CHARACTERS, INCLUDING ME!

FIRST, I INTRODUCE YOU TO THE BRIGHTEST AND MOST ROMANTIC OBJECT IN THE NIGHTTIME SKY... THE MOON.

THEN WE JOURNEY THROUGH OUR SOLAR SYSTEM, TO MEET THE SUN AND ITS FAMILY OF PLANETS.

NEXT, WE TRAVEL INTO THE STARLIT NIGHT FOR AN INTRODUCTION TO... WHO ELSE... THE STARS! WE LEARN HOW TO FIND THEM, ABOUT THE PATTERNS THEY MAKE WITH EACH OTHER, AND ABOUT HOW TO SEE THE BEST STAR SHOW EACH SEASON. WE ALSO LEARN ABOUT THE INTERESTING RELATIONSHIPS THAT THE STARS HAVE HAD WITH HUMANS OVER TIME.

THEN IT'S ON TO A TREASURE TROVE OF STARGAZING TIPS AND ASTRO-FACTS, PLUS WE SHOW YOU HOW TO BUILD A SIMPLE STAR VIEWER.

THE BOOK ENDS ON A GRAND COSMIC SCALE. YOU'LL BEGIN TO THINK ABOUT WHAT YOU'VE LEARNED FROM A UNIVERSAL PERSPECTIVE. HOW IMMENSE THE UNIVERSE REALLY IS!

OF COURSE, THIS BOOK CONTAINS ONLY **SOME** OF THE WONDERS VISIBLE TO THE NAKED EYE ON CLEAR DARK NIGHTS. THE SKY AND THIS UNIVERSE ARE FILLED WITH A BOUNDLESS SOURCE OF MAGIC AND WONDER.

THAT'S WHY THERE'S ALWAYS SOMETHING ABSOLUTELY AWESOME TO SEE... SO LOOK UP!

THE MYSTERIOUS MOON — 5

OUR SUN AND ITS FAMILY OF PLANETS — 14

THE BRIGHT STARS AND THE PATTERNS THEY MAKE — 24

SEASONAL STAR WATCHING
SPRING — 33
SUMMER — 38
AUTUMN — 44
WINTER — 55

SOME OBSERVING TIPS AND FACTS — 69

HOW TO USE THE ALL-SKY CHARTS — 76

FAREWELL — 81

GLOSSARY — 82

INDEX — 84

ABOUT THE AUTHORS/ILLUSTRATOR — 86

MOON AND MOONTH

OLD MOON IN THE NEW MOON'S ARMS

GREETINGS, GREETINGS, FELLOW STARGAZERS! I'D LIKE TO TELL YOU ABOUT AN OBJECT OF TRULY UNEARTHLY BEAUTY.

HAVE YOU EVER SEEN A VERY SLENDER CRESCENT MOON, GLOWING BRIGHTLY, WITH A DIM AND DARK, NEAR-FULL MOON TUCKED INSIDE THE CRESCENT?

FOR CENTURIES, THIS PHENOMENON HAS BEEN CALLED POETICALLY "THE OLD MOON IN THE NEW MOON'S ARMS."

HOW COME THE DARK, ALMOST-FULL OLD MOON SHINES WITH A PALE-GRAYISH GLOW? WELL, WE KNOW THAT ALL THE PLANETS AND THE MOON SHINE, NOT BY THEIR OWN LIGHT, BUT BY REFLECTED SUNLIGHT.

BUT THE PALE-GRAYISH GLOW IN THE YOUNG CRESCENT MOON'S ARMS IS ACTUALLY SUNLIGHT BOUNCING OFF OUR EARTH, THEN ON TO THE MOON, AND THEN REFLECTING BACK TOWARD US ONCE AGAIN.

ASTRONOMERS CALL THIS PALE-GRAYISH GLOW IN THE YOUNG CRESCENT MOON'S ARMS "EARTH SHINE"!

NOW, IF YOU WERE STANDING ON THE DARK PART OF THE MOON AND WERE LOOKING BACK AT EARTH, WHAT WOULD YOU SEE?

WELL, YOU WOULD SEE A NEAR-FULL EARTH, JUST THE OPPOSITE OF HOW WE SEE THE MOON! IF THE MOON WERE NEAR FULL, THEN THE EARTH FROM THE MOON WOULD APPEAR AS A VERY THIN CRESCENT.

SO REMEMBER, WHENEVER YOU SEE A CRESCENT MOON WITH "EARTHSHINE" THE CRESCENT IS BRILLIANT SUNSHINE BOUNCING DIRECTLY OFF THAT PORTION OF THE MOON, WHEREAS THE DARKER PART IS BEING LIT BY LIGHT REFLECTING OFF THE EARTH. IT'S EASY TO UNDERSTAND, IF YOU KEEP LOOKING UP!

A MOON/CAT TALE

TODAY, WE KNOW WHY THE MOON CHANGES ITS PHASE FROM NIGHT TO NIGHT.

BUT OUR ANCIENT ANCESTORS DIDN'T. IN FACT, THE EGYPTIANS THOUGHT IT ALL HAD TO DO WITH A **CAT**.

YOU SEE IT TAKES TWO WEEKS FOR THE SLIVERLIKE EYE OF THE YOUNG MOON TO OPEN WIDE TO FULL PHASE.

IT'S A HARDLY NOTICED, SLOW BUT GRADUAL AWAKENING OF EARTH'S CELESTIAL COMPANION.

NOW, AS YOU GAZE UP AT THIS YOUNG MOON, TRANSPORT YOURSELF BACK IN TIME 4,000 YEARS TO ANCIENT EGYPT

IMAGINE A PHARAOH, HIS COURT, AND HIS PRIESTS WAITING FOR THE SUN TO SET, THEIR BACKS TO THE NEWLY BUILT PYRAMIDS.

THE SUN'S LAST RAYS GLINT OFF THE HUGE STONE MONUMENTS.

THEN, AS THE SKY DARKENS, THE CRESCENT MOON WORSHIPED BY THESE PEOPLE AS THE MOON/CAT GODDESS MAKES ITS APPEARANCE.

CLAP CLAP CLAP

WHY A **CAT** GODDESS? BECAUSE, A CAT'S EYES CHANGE FROM NARROW SLITS TO FULL ORBS AS LIGHT CONDITIONS CHANGE, MIMICKING THE MOON'S TRANSFORMATION FROM CRESCENT TO FULL ORB.

YOU CAN SEE THIS IF YOU HOLD UP YOUR CAT AND FACE HIM OR HER TOWARD THE FULL MOON. YOUR CAT'S EYES WILL GO FROM BEING WIDE-OPEN IN THE DARK TO NARROW SLITS AS THEY ENCOUNTER THE MOON'S BRIGHTNESS.

IT'S AS IF THE CAT IS WINKING AT **ITS** CELESTIAL COMPANION!

MAYBE I'LL NAME MY CAT "MOONIE."

WINK!

 9

GREETINGS, GREETINGS, FELLOW STARGAZERS. EVER WONDER WHY THE FULL MOON LOOKS LARGER WHEN IT RISES THAN WHEN IT'S OVERHEAD?

JACK RABBIT

JACK

WELL, IT'S ONLY AN OPTICAL ILLUSION. AND YOU CAN PROVE IT TO YOURSELF. HOW?

SQUINT

THE NEXT TIME A FULL MOON RISES, SIMPLY TAKE A DIME AND HOLD IT AT ARM'S LENGTH.

SNATCH

I GUARANTEE THAT THE DIME WILL COVER EXACTLY THE SAME AMOUNT OF THE MOON... WHETHER THE MOON IS ON THE HORIZON OR OVERHEAD.

YOU SEE, WHEN THE MOON IS CLOSE TO FAMILIAR FOREGROUND OBJECTS, SUCH AS TREES AND BUILDINGS, IT LOOKS BIGGER.

IF, HOWEVER, THERE ARE NO FOREGROUND OBJECTS, OR IF THE FOREGROUND OBJECTS ARE TOTALLY UNFAMILIAR TO YOU OR STRANGE, THE MOON WILL ALMOST MAGICALLY SHRINK.

FOOMP

STILL DON'T BELIEVE ME THAT IT'S ALL AN OPTICAL ILLUSION? WELL, TRY THIS...

WINK

BEND OVER AT THE WAIST AND LOOK AT THE RISING FULL MOON UPSIDE DOWN BETWEEN YOUR LEGS!

THE MOON WILL LOOK SMALLER BECAUSE THE FAMILIAR TREES AND BUILDINGS WILL BE SEEN IN A WAY...

HARRINGTON

"...THAT MAKES THEM UNFAMILIAR.

TRY IT! IT'S AMAZING, AND IT'S FUN!

THE HARVEST AND JACK-O'-LANTERN MOON

GREETINGS, GREETINGS, FELLOW STARGAZERS! DID YOU KNOW THAT THE HARVEST MOON IS NOT AN ORANGE MOON? NOR IS IT NECESSARILY A **BIG** MOON...

THE HARVEST MOON IS THE NAME GIVEN TO THE FULL MOON CLOSEST TO THE TIME OF THE AUTUMNAL EQUINOX, WHICH HAPPENS EACH SEPTEMBER.

WHY? WELL, LET'S GET BASIC. A "HARVEST," ACCORDING TO THE DICTIONARY, IS SIMPLY THE ACT OF GATHERING A CROP. SO, THE FULL MOON CLOSEST TO THE FIRST DAY OF FALL, THE AUTUMNAL EQUINOX, WAS CALLED THE HARVEST MOON.

THE ECLIPTIC PATH OF THE HARVEST MOON MAKES A MUCH SMALLER ANGLE WITH THE HORIZON NOW THAN AT ANY OTHER TIME OF THE YEAR. THAT MEANS A REALLY BRIGHT MOON WILL RISE CLOSE TO SUNSET FOR SEVERAL NIGHTS IN A ROW!

THIS BIT OF ASTRONOMICAL "WIZARDRY" MEANT A LOT TO FARMERS BEFORE THE INVENTION OF ELECTRIC LIGHTS. THEY COULD HARVEST THEIR CROPS AFTER SUNSET FOR SEVERAL EVENINGS BY THE BRIGHT LIGHT OF THE MOON!

BUT HOW DID THE COLOR ORANGE BECOME ASSOCIATED WITH THE HARVEST MOON?

WELL, WHENEVER **ANY** FULL MOON IS CLOSE TO THE HORIZON, WE SEE IT THROUGH THICKER AND DUSTIER LAYERS OF EARTH'S ATMOSPHERE. THE DUSTIER THE ATMOSPHERE, THE MORE ORANGE THE MOON LOOKS... JUST LIKE THE RISING OR SETTING SUN UNDER SIMILAR CONDITIONS.

WHEN THERE'S AN ORANGE FULL MOON ON HALLOWEEN, ALMOST EVERYONE REMARKS THAT IT LOOKS LIKE A JACK-O'-LANTERN.

SUCH A SIGHT LONG AGO MAY HAVE PROMPTED PEOPLE TO CARVE FACES ON THEIR HALLOWEEN PUMPKINS.

SO OUR JACK-O'-LANTERN TRADITION MAY HAVE ORIGINATED WITH AN IMAGINED FACE ON AN ANCIENT MOON... OUR MAN IN THE MOON.

LADY MOON AND A RABBIT

Is it a man in the moon... or is it a lady? Let's investigate.

Anyone who looks at the moon will agree that it is not a disk of pure white light.

IT'S NOT PURE

YOU'RE RIGHT

That's right! The moon has dark patches that early astronomers called *MARIA*, meaning "seas".

GLUG GLUG

Today, we know that the moon's "seas" are really frozen lava flows.

FOOMP

But this doesn't stop us from seeing those dark markings as all kinds of fanciful shapes, such as the man in the moon, or a jack-o'-lantern.

But none is more beautiful than the profile of the lady in the moon.

FOR ME?

She's best seen when the moon is full and high in the sky. Look for a flower in her hair and a pearl necklace.

Now, if you really want to use your imagination, get up before sunrise and look at the full moon in the west just before it sets.

If you do, you will see that the lady has turned into a rabbit.

I love the moon, because its dark markings are a playground for the imagination, if you keep looking up!

HARRINGTON

BLUE MOON AND GREEN CHEESE

GREETINGS, GREETINGS, FELLOW STARGAZERS! IT HAS BECOME COMMON KNOWLEDGE THAT THE BLUE MOON IS THE SECOND FULL MOON IN ANY ONE MONTH. AND THAT HAPPENS ABOUT ONCE EVERY 2.72 YEARS.

BUT THAT'S NOT WHAT I WANT TO TALK ABOUT. YOU SEE, THE **REAL** BLUE MOON IS THOUGHT TO DERIVE FROM COMMON LANGUAGE EXPRESSIONS USED WELL OVER 400 YEARS AGO.

M'LADY..

M'LORD..

LONG AGO, SENTENCES THAT INCLUDED REFERENCES TO A "BLUE MOON" OR TO A MOON MADE OF "GREEN CHEESE" MEANT THAT THERE WAS AN OBVIOUS ABSURDITY AT HAND: "HE THINKS THE MOON IS BLUE" OR "SHE TALKS AS IF THE MOON WERE MADE OF GREEN CHEESE".

EVENTUALLY, THESE TWO MOON PHRASES ADOPTED A SECOND MEANING, THAT OF "NEVER": "I TELL YOU, THAT SHIP WILL RETURN WHEN THE MOON TURNS BLUE!" WAS LIKE SAYING THAT IT WOULD HAPPEN ON THE TWELFTH OF NEVER. OR, SIMPLY, **NEVER!**

ARRRR

ARRRR

YET, THE MOON **CAN** ACTUALLY TURN BLUE, ESPECIALLY AFTER MAJOR VOLCANIC ERUPTIONS AND FOREST FIRES. THE SMOKY PARTICLES AND GASES LEFT IN THE SKY CAN BE OF JUST THE RIGHT SIZE TO SCATTER AWAY RED LIGHT, LEAVING AN EXCESS OF BLUE LIGHT. BLUE MOONS WERE SEEN FOR TWO YEARS AFTER THE 1883 KRAKATAU ERUPTION IN INDONESIA

SLOOP JACK B.

OF COURSE, THESE EVENTS HAPPEN ONLY "ONCE IN A BLUE MOON". TO CATCH THEM, YOU HAVE TO KEEP LOOKING UP!

HARRINGTON

SATURN
6
NEPTUNE
8
EARTH
3
MERCURY
1
9
PLUTO
7
URANUS
4
MARS
2
VENUS
5
JUPITER

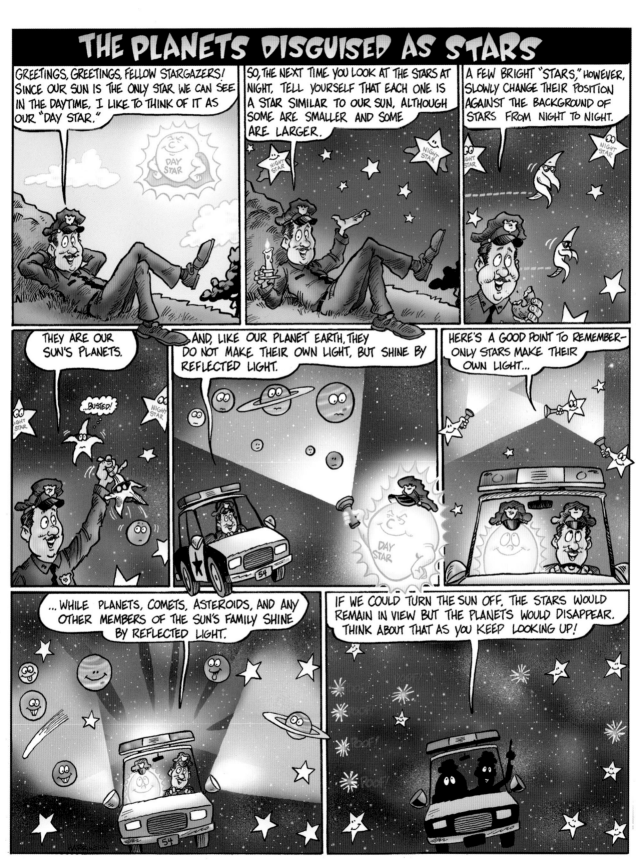

THE PLANETS DISGUISED AS STARS

GREETINGS, GREETINGS, FELLOW STARGAZERS! SINCE OUR SUN IS THE ONLY STAR WE CAN SEE IN THE DAYTIME, I LIKE TO THINK OF IT AS OUR "DAY STAR."

SO, THE NEXT TIME YOU LOOK AT THE STARS AT NIGHT, TELL YOURSELF THAT EACH ONE IS A STAR SIMILAR TO OUR SUN, ALTHOUGH SOME ARE SMALLER AND SOME ARE LARGER.

A FEW BRIGHT "STARS," HOWEVER, SLOWLY CHANGE THEIR POSITION AGAINST THE BACKGROUND OF STARS FROM NIGHT TO NIGHT.

THEY ARE OUR SUN'S PLANETS.

AND, LIKE OUR PLANET EARTH, THEY DO NOT MAKE THEIR OWN LIGHT, BUT SHINE BY REFLECTED LIGHT.

HERE'S A GOOD POINT TO REMEMBER— ONLY STARS MAKE THEIR OWN LIGHT...

...WHILE PLANETS, COMETS, ASTEROIDS, AND ANY OTHER MEMBERS OF THE SUN'S FAMILY SHINE BY REFLECTED LIGHT.

IF WE COULD TURN THE SUN OFF, THE STARS WOULD REMAIN IN VIEW BUT THE PLANETS WOULD DISAPPEAR. THINK ABOUT THAT AS YOU KEEP LOOKING UP!

THE PINK IRON PLANET AND THE EARTH'S TWIN

GREETINGS, GREETINGS, FELLOW STARGAZERS. MERCURY AND VENUS ORBIT SO CLOSE TO THE SUN THAT WE CANNOT SEE EITHER OF THEM VERY LATE AT NIGHT.

ESPECIALLY MERCURY, WHICH LOOKS PINK BECAUSE WE SEE IT THROUGH THE DUSTIEST LAYERS OF OUR ATMOSPHERE!

MERCURY IS TINY... ONLY ABOUT THE SIZE OF OUR MOON. IT'S SOMETIMES CALLED THE PINK IRON PLANET BECAUSE IT CONTAINS MORE IRON THAN OUR ENTIRE EARTH!

HEY!

SLURP SLURP SLURP

NOW, VENUS IS THE TWIN SISTER OF EARTH. THAT'S BECAUSE IT IS ALMOST EXACTLY THE SAME SIZE.

VENUS IS ALSO THE BRIGHTEST OF ALL THE PLANETS BECAUSE IT IS COMPLETELY COVERED WITH HIGHLY REFLECTIVE CLOUDS.

BUT THIS PLANET-WIDE CLOUD COVER IS SO HEAVY THAT YOU'D BE SQUASHED FLATTER THAN A PANCAKE IF YOU WERE ON VENUS'S SURFACE.

WELCOME TO VENUS

TEMPERATURES ARE RATHER UNPLEASANT ALSO—ALMOST 1,000 DEGREES FAHRENHEIT... HOT ENOUGH TO MELT LEAD!

DANGER

ON TOP OF WHICH, IT RAINS SULFURIC ACID! VENUS IS BEAUTIFUL TO LOOK AT FROM AFAR, BUT NOT A NICE PLACE TO VISIT.

TOTO, I DON'T THINK WE'RE IN KANSAS ANYMORE...

I'M NOT TOTO, SWEETIE...

SO ENJOY YOUR VIEWS OF VENUS, OUR MOST BRILLIANT EVENING "STAR" WHEN IT APPEARS AFTER SUNSET,

WEST

AND OUR MOST BRILLIANT MORNING "STAR" WHEN IT APPEARS BEFORE SUNRISE.

EAST

AND, DON'T FORGET: THROUGH A TELESCOPE, YOU CAN WATCH VENUS AND MERCURY GO THROUGH PHASES JUST LIKE OUR MOON – IF YOU KEEP LOOKING UP!

VISIBLE IN THE EVENING | NOT VISIBLE FROM EARTH | VISIBLE IN THE MORNING

GIBBOUS · HALF · MERCURY · GIBBOUS · HALF · VENUS · EARTH

HARRINGTON

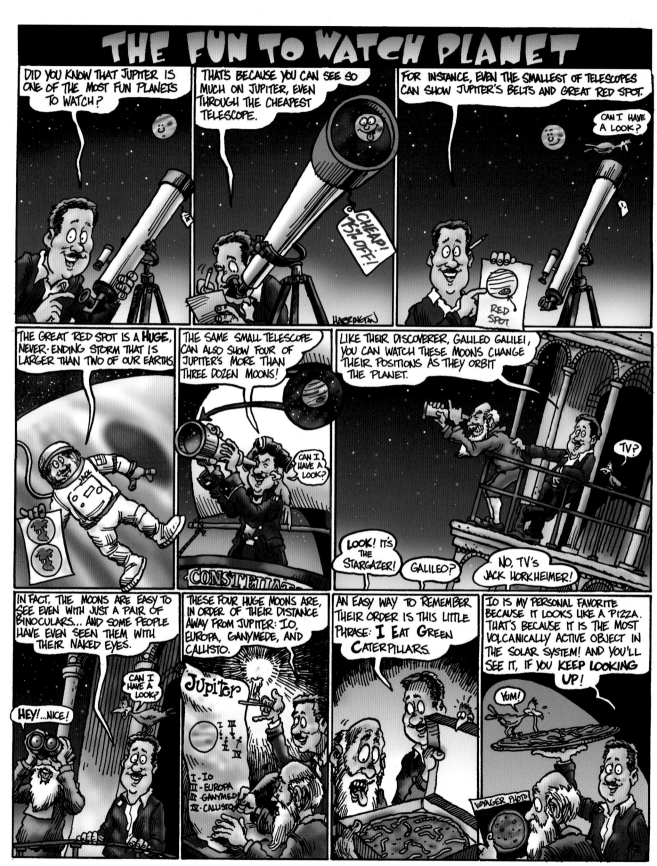

IS JUPITER KING OF THE PLANETS?

GREETINGS, GREETINGS, FELLOW STAR AND PLANET GAZERS! THE BIGGEST PLANET IN OUR SOLAR SYSTEM IS JUPITER, FOLLOWED BY SATURN. BUT I WOULD LIKE TO CLARIFY SOMETHING ABOUT JUPITER AND SATURN.

JUPITER IS CALLED THE KING OF THE PLANETS BECAUSE IT'S 13,000 MILES WIDER THAN 75,000-MILE-WIDE SATURN, SO IT IS ABOUT 15 PERCENT LARGER.

88,000 MILES

75,000 MILES

BUT IF WE MEASURE SATURN FROM ONE EDGE OF ITS RING SYSTEM TO THE OTHER EDGE, WE DISCOVER THAT SATURN'S RING SYSTEM IS 176,000 MILES WIDE — EXACTLY TWO TIMES THE WIDTH OF JUPITER!

176,000 MILES

THAT MEANS WE COULD LINE UP TWO JUPITERS SIDE-BY-SIDE FROM ONE EDGE OF SATURN'S RINGS TO THE OTHER.

BUT SATURN'S RINGS DON'T COUNT WHEN WE REFER TO PLANET SIZE, SO JUPITER REMAINS THE KING. BESIDES, JUPITER HAS A VERY DIM RING, TOO. BUT, SINCE SATURN IS A FAVORITE OF MINE, I LIKE TO THINK THAT SATURN'S REALLY THE LARGEST PLANET.

EVEN SO, YOU MIGHT EXPECT THAT SATURN, WITH ITS RINGS, WOULD LOOK ALMOST TWICE AS WIDE AS JUPITER THROUGH A SMALL TELESCOPE. BUT IT DOESN'T! IN FACT, SATURN LOOKS ALMOST TWO TIMES SMALLER!

THE REASON IS SIMPLE: SATURN IS TWICE AS FAR AWAY. YOU SEE, WHILE JUPITER IS ONLY 500 MILLION MILES AWAY FROM THE SUN, SATURN IS 1 BILLION MILES FROM OUR STAR.

PUFF PUFF

WELL, AT ANY RATE, I HOPE YOU GET TO EXPERIENCE SATURN SOMETIME THROUGH A TELESCOPE BECAUSE, DESPITE ITS SIZE, IT'S ONE OF THE MOST BEAUTIFUL SIGHTS IN THE NIGHT SKY. AND YOU WILL, IF YOU KEEP LOOKING UP!

CURIOUS PLANET GEORGE

GREETINGS, GREETINGS, FELLOW PLANET LOVERS, I'M "CURIOUS". HAVE YOU EVER HEARD OF A PLANET NAMED GEORGE?

IT'S TRUE, BELIEVE IT OR NOT, THERE'S A TINY, GREENISH-BLUE "STAR" OUT THERE IN THE HEAVENS, WHICH CAN BE SEEN IN BINOCULARS, AND WHOSE NAME WAS, IN FACT, ONE TIME, GEORGE.

THAT LITTLE "STAR" IS ACTUALLY A PLANET 4 TIMES THE DIAMETER OF THE EARTH AND 8 TIMES THE DIAMETER OF MARS. IT'S A 32,000-MILE-WIDE PLANET ALMOST 2 BILLION MILES AWAY.

GEORGE WAS DISCOVERED ONLY 200 YEARS AGO, IN 1781, AT THE TIME OF THE AMERICAN REVOLUTION. IT WAS NAMED BY ITS DISCOVERER FOR THE VERY KING WHO WAS ONE OF THE CAUSES OF THE AMERICAN REVOLUTION, KING GEORGE THE THIRD OF ENGLAND.

INDEED, WHEN ENGLISHMAN SIR WILLIAM HERSCHEL DISCOVERED THIS PLANET, HE NAMED IT "GEORGIUM SIDUS," WHICH TRANSLATED FROM THE LATIN MEANS "GEORGE'S STAR."

GEORGIUM SIDUS

BUT OTHER ASTRONOMERS AT THE TIME DIDN'T LIKE THE IDEA OF POLITICIZING THE HEAVENS, SO THEY QUICKLY RENAMED IT HERSCHEL, AFTER ITS DISCOVERER, A NAME THAT YOU CAN STILL FIND IN MANY ASTRONOMY BOOKS OF THE LAST CENTURY.

POW!

GEORGIUM SIDUS HERSCHEL

BUT THEN A BIG BROUHAHA ENSUED, AND TWO OTHER ASTRONOMERS CLAIMED THEY HAD SEEN IT BEFORE HERSCHEL, ALTHOUGH THEY ADMITTED THEY DIDN'T KNOW WHAT IT WAS.

ALL THIS RESULTED IN A COSMIC TEMPEST IN A TEAPOT, WHICH FINALLY ENDED WITH THE PLANET BEING RENAMED AGAIN FOR THE GREEK GOD OF THE SKY, URANUS. ASTRONOMERS SAID THIS NAME WAS MUCH MORE IN KEEPING WITH THE MYTHOLOGICAL NAMES OF THE OTHER PLANETS.

GEORGIUM SIDUS HERSCHEL URANUS

SO NOW YOU KNOW HOW CURIOUS PLANET GEORGE WAS RENAMED HERSCHEL, THEN RENAMED URANUS! IT'S ALL A MATTER OF CELESTIAL POLITICS, WHICH YOU'LL UNDERSTAND IF YOU KEEP LOOKING UP!

BAM!

GEORGE

URANUS

THE PLANET THAT WENT "TILT" AND OTHER FAR-OUT PLANETS

URANUS IS A WEIRD PLANET IN MANY WAYS.

LIKE JUPITER AND SATURN, URANUS IS A GAS GIANT PLANET, MEANING THAT IT HAS A TINY CORE SURROUNDED BY MANY LAYERS OF GAS.

URANUS IS NOT NEARLY AS LARGE AS JUPITER. WE COULD FIT ONLY ABOUT FOUR EARTHS ACROSS ITS FACE.

BUT URANUS IS STRANGE... IT IS A PLANET THAT WENT "TILT." IN FACT, IT ORBITS THE SUN ON ITS SIDE...

...WHICH MEANS THAT SOMETIMES ITS NORTH POLE IS POINTED DIRECTLY AT THE SUN AND SOMETIMES ITS SOUTH POLE IS.

NEPTUNE IS ONLY SLIGHTLY LARGER THAN URANUS AND IS ANOTHER GAS GIANT, BUT IT IS NOT TILTED ON ITS SIDE.

NEPTUNE WAS DISCOVERED IN 1846, AFTER ASTRONOMERS PREDICTED ITS EXISTENCE MATHEMATICALLY.

YOU SEE, ASTRONOMERS SAW THE INVISIBLE PULL OF NEPTUNE'S GRAVITY ON URANUS, WHICH MADE URANUS MOVE IN A FUNNY WAY IN ITS ORBIT.

HAW!

THE SEARCH FOR TINY PLUTO ALSO BEGAN WITH A TUG... ALMOST IMPERCEPTIBLE... THIS TIME ON NEPTUNE. HOWEVER, IT ENDED IN 1930 WHEN CLYDE TOMBAUGH SAW THE TINY PLANET FOR THE FIRST TIME IN PHOTOGRAPHS!

WE NOW KNOW THAT PLUTO HAS A MOON, CHARON, WHICH IS ALMOST AS LARGE AS THE PLANET ITSELF, SO WE SOMETIMES CALL PLUTO A DOUBLE PLANET.

THAT'S THE STORY OF THE OUTER PLANETS. THERE'S SO MUCH TO LEARN IF YOU KEEP LOOKING UP!

JUST WHAT IS A STAR, ANYWAY?

GREETINGS, GREETINGS, FELLOW STARGAZERS. HAVE YOU EVER WONDERED JUST WHAT A STAR **IS**?

WELL, LET ME "UN-WONDER" YOU.

HEH! HEH!

IF YOU WERE OUTSIDE ON A CLEAR NIGHT LOOKING UP AT THE STARS, COULD YOU POINT OUT THE CLOSEST ONE?

ME!

OVER HERE!

SOME PEOPLE THINK THAT IT'S THE NORTH STAR... BUT NOTHING COULD BE FURTHER FROM THE TRUTH. ACTUALLY, IT'S OUR SUN!

DUDE! .... WHAT'S UPPPPP...

NORTH STAR RULES!

BAP!

OUR SUN IS THE CLOSEST STAR TO EARTH – AND THEREFORE THE BRIGHTEST TO US. THE ONLY REASON THAT IT DOESN'T LOOK LIKE THE OTHER STARS AT NIGHT IS BECAUSE IT IS SO CLOSE.

JUST LIKE ME... THEY LONG TO BE... CLOSE TO YOUUUU...

THANK YOU, THANK YOU VERY MUCH...

SHOW-OFF...

AND THE REASON THAT THE OTHER STARS DON'T LOOK LIKE OUR SUN IS THAT THEY ARE SO INCREDIBLY MUCH FARTHER AWAY.

JACK! COME BACK! ....JACK!

HEY! OVER HERE!

HEY, JACK!

NOW, ALL THE STARS MAKE THEIR OWN LIGHT SIMILAR TO THE WAY OUR SUN DOES.

YOU SEE, OUR SUN AND ALL THE STARS ARE GIGANTIC BALLS OF HOT, GLOWING GAS.

HEY! WHO YOU CALLING A GAS BAG?

AND MOST OF THEM MAKE LIGHT BY THERMONUCLEAR PROCESSES. OR IF YOU LIKE TO THINK OF IT THIS WAY...

BY WHAT?

MATCH

OUR SUN PRODUCES MORE ENERGY EVERY SINGLE SECOND THAN SEVERAL MILLION HYDROGEN BOMBS DETONATING AT THE SAME TIME. IMAGINE HOW MUCH YOU CAN LEARN, IF YOU JUST KEEP LOOKING UP!

AND I THOUGHT IT WAS JUST AN UPSET STOMACH!

HARRINGTON

HOW FAR AWAY ARE THE STARS?

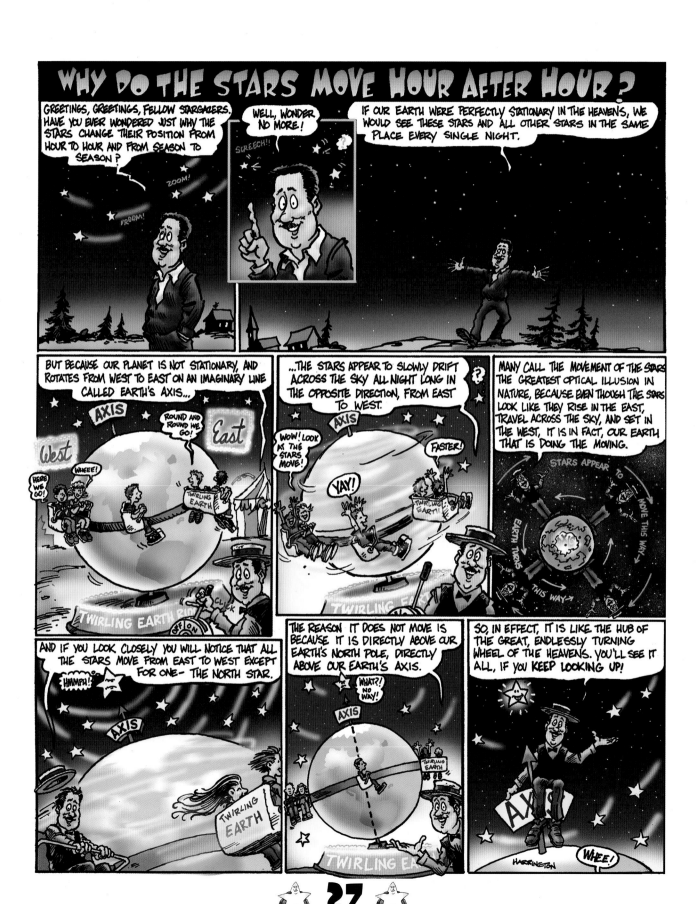

WHY THE STARS CHANGE WITH THE SEASONS

GREETINGS, GREETINGS, FELLOW STARGAZERS.

JUST AS WE HAVE SEASONS HERE ON EARTH, SO TOO DO THE HEAVENS HAVE THEIR SEASONS. WHY?

OKAY. YOU KNOW THAT OUR EARTH ROTATES ONCE EVERY 24 HOURS FROM WEST TO EAST.

EAST

WEST

THAT MOTION CAUSES THE STARS TO APPEAR TO MOVE ACROSS THE SKY FROM EAST TO WEST.

EAST

WEST

BUT EARTH ALSO JOURNEYS AROUND THE SUN ONCE EVERY 365¼ DAYS.

SO OUR VIEW OF THE NIGHT SKY ALSO CHANGES AS WE ORBIT THE SUN.

HOW DO WE SEE THE SKY CHANGE AFTER 90 DAYS, WHICH IS A QUARTER OF A YEAR?

WELL, ANY STAR THAT WAS ON THE HORIZON AT 8 P.M. ON DAY 1 WILL HAVE MOVED A QUARTER OF THE WAY AROUND THE ENTIRE OBSERVABLE SKY BY 8 P.M. ON DAY 90.

DAY 1

STAR EVIDENCE "A"

DAY 90

STAR EVIDENCE "A"

STAR EVIDENCE "B"

EAST

EAST

AND SINCE EACH SEASON IS A QUARTER OF A YEAR LONG, THE STARS THAT WE SEE OVERHEAD IN EARLY EVENING DURING ONE SEASON...

DAY 90

STAR EVIDENCE "A"

STAR EVIDENCE "B"

EAST

WILL NOT BE THE SAME STARS WE SEE OVERHEAD IN EARLY EVENING DURING THE PREVIOUS OR FOLLOWING SEASONS. YOU SEE, IT'S ELEMENTARY, IF YOU KEEP LOOKING UP!

DAY 180

STAR EVIDENCE "B"

STAR EVIDENCE "C"

STAR EVIDENCE "A"

EAST

WEST

THE TRUTH ABOUT THE NORTH STAR

GREETINGS, GREETINGS, FELLOW STARGAZERS! WHAT'S THE BRIGHTEST STAR IN THE NIGHT SKY?

WELL, IF YOU SAID THE NORTH STAR, YOU'RE WRONG. IT'S SIRIUS. MOST PEOPLE ACTUALLY BELIEVE THAT THE NORTH STAR IS THE BRIGHTEST STAR, WHEN IN FACT THERE ARE 45 OTHER STARS VISIBLE TO THE NAKED EYE THAT ARE BRIGHTER.

MANY PEOPLE THINK THE NORTH STAR IS THE BRIGHTEST STAR BECAUSE THEY HEAR SO MUCH ABOUT ITS IMPORTANCE TO HUMANKIND.

YOU SEE, THE NORTH STAR IS ALSO CALLED POLARIS BECAUSE IT IS THE CLOSEST BRIGHT STAR TO THE NORTH CELESTIAL POLE.

WHICH MEANS THAT IF WE COULD STAND AT THE NORTH POLE, THE NORTH STAR OR POLARIS WOULD BE DIRECTLY OVERHEAD—DIRECTLY ABOVE THE EARTH'S AXIS.

NOW, IF YOU THINK OF THE EARTH'S AXIS AS A HUGE NAIL THAT WE COULD INSERT AT THE SOUTH POLE, AND IF WE PUSHED IT ALL THE WAY THROUGH THE PLANET AND HAD IT COME OUT AT THE NORTH POLE AND EXTEND INTO SPACE, THE NAIL WOULD POINT TO THE NORTH STAR.

SO, AS THE EARTH TURNS ON ITS AXIS, ALL THE STARS IN THE HEAVENS SEEM TO MOVE, EXCEPT ONE... THE STAR DIRECTLY ABOVE THE EARTH'S AXIS, POLARIS, THE NORTH STAR.

YOU SEE, THE NORTH STAR IS THE ONLY STAR THAT REMAINS STATIONARY IN THE HEAVENS. THAT'S WHY IT HAS BEEN SO IMPORTANT. BEFORE THE INVENTION OF THE COMPASS, THIS STAR WAS EXTREMELY IMPORTANT IN HELPING NAVIGATORS AND EXPLORERS DETERMINE DIRECTION.

FOR AS LONG AS YOU LIVE, THE NORTH STAR WILL ALWAYS BE DUE NORTH, AND IF IT'S NOT, YOU'RE ON THE WRONG PLANET, WHICH ISN'T LIKELY, IF YOU KEEP LOOKING UP!

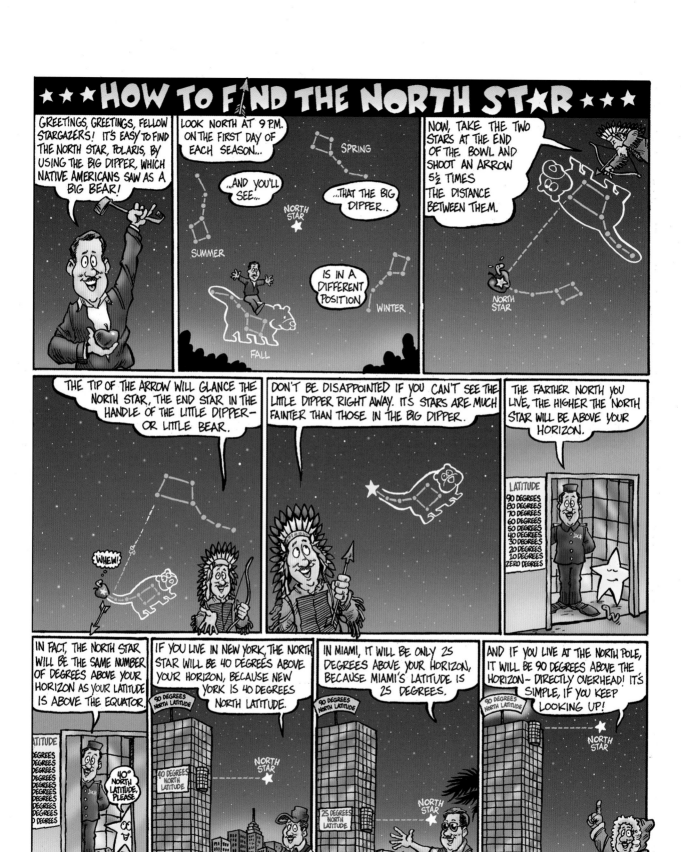

GREETINGS, GREETINGS, FELLOW STARGAZERS. GET YOUR SADDLE READY. WE'RE GOING TO RIDE THE HORSE IN THE BIG DIPPER!

WHERE'S THE HORSE, YOU ASK?

OKAY, LOOK AT THE THREE STARS THAT MAKE UP THE BIG DIPPER'S HANDLE. SEE THE STAR AT THE BEND OF THE HANDLE, NAMED MIZAR?

WELL, MIZAR HAS A SECRET. IF YOU LOOK REALLY CLOSE AT THE STAR, YOU'LL SEE THAT IT IS NOT JUST ONE STAR, BUT TWO!

ITS DIMMER COMPANION IS ALCOR, WHICH IN ARABIC MEANS "THE LOST OR FRIENDLESS ONE."

HEE HEE

CENTURIES AGO, ONE ARABIAN ARMY USED BRIGHT MIZAR AND DIMMER ALCOR AS A KIND OF EYE EXAM. IF A RECRUIT COULD SEE THE TWO STARS, HE WAS IN. IF HE COULDN'T, HE WAS OUT.

ONE!...NO, WAIT— TWO. HMM...NO, ONE.

DO YOU SEE IT?

LONG AGO, THESE TWO STARS WERE KNOWN AS "THE HORSE AND THE RIDER"— MIZAR BEING THE HORSE, AND ALCOR, THE RIDER.

BUT THE MAGIC DOESN'T END THERE! MODERN ASTRONOMERS HAVE DISCOVERED THAT TOGETHER MIZAR AND ALCOR FORM A RARE QUINTUPLE STAR.

MIZAR, THE HORSE, IS NOT JUST ONE, OR TWO, OR THREE, BUT FOUR STARS. WOW!

ISN'T IT INCREDIBLE WHAT MODERN ASTRONOMY CAN REVEAL ABOUT OBJECTS THAT GENERATIONS OF HUMANS HAVE SEEN FOR THOUSANDS OF YEARS? SO, KEEP LOOKING UP!

SPRING

LOW LYIN' ORION AND THE HIGH FLYIN' LION

GREETINGS, GREETINGS, FELLOW STARGAZERS. IT'S THAT TIME OF YEAR AGAIN WHEN THE SKIES EXCLAIM "SPRING IS HERE!"

INDEED, IF YOU GO OUT ANY CLEAR NIGHT IN EARLY EVENING AT THE END OF MARCH AND BEGINNING OF APRIL, YOU WILL SEE A CELESTIAL ANNOUNCEMENT OF SPRING — AN ARRANGEMENT OF STARS THAT I CALL LOW LYIN' ORION AND THE HIGH FLYIN' LION. I'LL EXPLAIN.

THE STAR PATTERN ORION, THE HUNTER, IS THE SUREST SKY SIGN OF WINTER. IN JANUARY AND FEBRUARY, WHEN WINTER IS COLDEST, ORION REACHES HIS HIGHEST POINT IN THE HEAVENS AT AROUND 9 P.M. — BRAGGING THAT HE IS THE MASTER OF THE SEASON.

SOUTH

AS WINTER TURNS TO SPRING, ORION LEAVES CENTER STAGE, CREEPING FARTHER WEST EACH NIGHT. COME LATE MARCH, HE IS TIPPED OVER ON HIS SIDE, SLIDING DOWN IN THE SOUTHWEST, HANGING ON FOR DEAR LIFE AND REMINDING US THAT A FEW COLD DAYS REMAIN AS LONG AS HE'S AROUND.

WHOOPS!

SOUTHWEST

AND ALTHOUGH I'M ALWAYS SAD TO SEE ORION'S BRIGHT STARS GO, A LESS BRIGHT BUT MUCH BIGGER CONSTELLATION TAKES HIS PLACE.

SO LONG

CROUCHED ALMOST OVERHEAD, THE CONSTELLATION LEO, THE LION, ROARS — LETTING US KNOW THAT HIS SEASON, SPRING, IS HERE.

SPRING IS HERE!

NOTICE THAT THE FRONT PART OF LEO IS MARKED BY A BACKWARD QUESTION MARK OR SICKLE. THE BRIGHT STAR REGULUS MARKS HIS HEART, AND A TRIANGLE OF STARS TO THE EAST MARKS HIS TAIL END.

SO WHY DO I CALL THIS THE TIME OF LOW LYIN' ORION AND THE HIGH FLYIN' LION?

WELL, IT SPEAKS FOR ITSELF. LEO, THE LION, IS INDEED FLYIN' HIGH OVERHEAD, AND ORION IS NOT ONLY LYIN' LOW IN THE SKY, BUT ALSO HAS A REPUTATION AS ONE OF THE BIGGEST COSMIC LIARS IN MYTHOLOGY.

KRAK!

SO, GET OUT UNDER THESE EXQUISITE EARLY EVENING SPRING SKIES TO SEE TWO FABULOUS CONSTELLATIONS... AND, OF COURSE, **KEEP LOOKING UP!**

WHY IS SPRING CALLED "SPRING"?

GREETINGS, GREETINGS, FELLOW STARGAZERS, AND HAPPY VERNAL EQUINOX! THAT'S WHAT ASTRONOMERS CALL THE FIRST DAY OF SPRING.

HAVE YOU EVER WONDERED WHY WE CALL SPRING "SPRING"?

WELL, THE WORD SPRING IS SIMPLY SHORT FOR THE PHRASES "SPRING OF THE LEAF" AND "SPRING OF THE YEAR."

"SPRING OF THE LEAF" IS PRETTY OBVIOUS. THAT'S THE TIME OF YEAR WHEN LEAVES LITERALLY SPRING OUT OF THE BRANCHES AND GRASS SPRINGS UP OUT OF THE GROUND.

BUT WHAT DOES "SPRING OF THE YEAR" MEAN?

WELL, BELIEVE IT OR NOT, UNTIL THE YEAR 1752, THE FIRST OF THE YEAR IN AMERICA AND IN ENGLAND WAS CELEBRATED ON MARCH 25TH! IN OTHER WORDS, THE NEW YEAR SPRANG UP AT THE SAME TIME AS THE LEAVES AND THE GRASS.

IN FACT, WHEN AMERICA'S FOUNDING FATHERS WERE YOUNG MEN, THEY ALL WISHED EACH OTHER HAPPY NEW YEAR ON MARCH 25TH -UNTIL PARLIAMENT DECLARED THAT THE NEW YEAR WOULD CHANGE TO JANUARY 1ST BEGINNING IN 1752.

AT ANY RATE, I PERSONALLY THINK IT'S MUCH MORE LOGICAL TO HAVE THE NEW YEAR BEGIN WITH THE BEGINNING OF SPRING WHEN ALL OF NATURE SEEMS TO BEGIN AGAIN, IT MAKES SENSE... IF YOU KEEP LOOKING UP!

34

GREETINGS, GREETINGS, FELLOW STARGAZERS AND BOY, DON'T YOU JUST LOVE SPRING? I ESPECIALLY ENJOY THE SOFT MUTED STARS OF SPRING THAT ECHO THE GENTLE COLORS OF EARTH'S LANDSCAPE!

YOU KNOW, I'VE ALWAYS BEEN FASCINATED BY FOLKLORE—ESPECIALLY PHRASES THAT WE LEARN DURING CHILDHOOD, THE ORIGINS OF WHICH WE HAVE LITTLE OR NO IDEA OF.

I'M SURE YOU'VE HEARD THAT OLD PHRASE ABOUT MARCH WEATHER THAT GOES "IN LIKE A LION, OUT LIKE A LAMB" AND VICE-VERSA. BUT WHERE DID THIS COME FROM?

WELL, IT APPEARS THIS PHRASE GOT ITS IMAGERY FROM THE HEAVENS!

IF YOU GO OUTSIDE ON MARCH 1st AT 8 P.M., AND LOOK ABOVE THE WESTERN HORIZON, YOU'LL SEE THE DIM STARS THAT MAKE UP ARIES, THE RAM OR LAMB.

BUT IF YOU LOOK ALMOST OPPOSITE, AT ABOUT THE SAME HEIGHT ABOVE THE HORIZON IN THE EAST, YOU'LL SEE THE CONSTELLATION LEO, THE LION.

SO, THE LION IS RISING INTO THE NIGHT SKY AT THE BEGINNING OF MARCH, WHICH SUPPORTS THE FACT THAT MARCH USUALLY BEGINS WITH FIERCER WEATHER.

ROAR RR!

WELL, ³AHEM≼...ONE MONTH LATER, ON MARCH 31st AT 8 P.M., HOWEVER, THE LION WILL BE ALMOST OVERHEAD AND THE LAMB WILL BE SMACK-DAB ON THE WESTERN HORIZON.

NOW, WE ALL KNOW THAT USUALLY THE WEATHER AT THE END OF MARCH IS MILDER THAN THE WEATHER AT THE BEGINNING OF MARCH, SO THE LAMB SETTING INDICATES THAT MARCH IS GOING OUT LIKE A LAMB!

SO PERHAPS LONG AGO SOMEONE TIED ALL THIS TOGETHER AND DECIDED TO POETICALLY LINK BOTH CONSTELLATIONS TO THE WEATHER, COMING UP WITH THAT OLD PHRASE. WHATEVER, MAY YOU ALWAYS HAVE CLEAR SKIES IN MARCH FOR VIEWING THE LION AND THE LAMB, WHICH IS EASY IF YOU REMEMBER TO KEEP LOOKING UP!

REGULUS AND DENEBOLA, THE HEART AND TAIL OF LEO, THE LION

GREETINGS, GREETINGS, FELLOW STARGAZERS. LET'S LOOK AT THE TWO BRIGHTEST STARS OF SPRING'S MOST PROMINENT CONSTELLATION, LEO, THE LION.

PURRRR...

ABOUT AN HOUR AFTER SUNSET, THE CELESTIAL KING OF BEASTS IS ABOUT HALFWAY UP THE WESTERN SKY.

LEO'S BRIGHTEST STAR, REGULUS, (OR LITTLE KING), MARKS THE LION'S HEART.

REGULUS

LEO'S SECOND-BRIGHTEST STAR IS DENEBOLA.

DENEBOLA

BUT DON'T CONFUSE DENEBOLA WITH DENEB, THE "TAIL" OF CYGNUS, THE SWAN.

CYGNUS   LEO

IN FACT, "DENEB" MEANS TAIL, AND "OLA" MEANS LION, SO DENEBOLA LITERALLY MEANS "TAIL OF THE LION".

NOW, DENEBOLA IS 36 LIGHT-YEARS AWAY. IT SHINES 12 TIMES BRIGHTER!

OUR SUN

1 MILLION MILES

DENEBOLA

REGULUS IS ABOUT TWICE AS FAR AWAY FROM US AS DENEBOLA. BUT IT APPEARS MUCH BRIGHTER. WHY?

$\sqrt{400} = 5$

BECAUSE REGULUS IS 3.5 TIMES THE DIAMETER OF OUR SUN AND SHINES 140 TIMES BRIGHTER! **WOW!**

REGULUS

DENEBOLA

WELL, BE SURE TO GO OUTSIDE AND SEE THE TRUE WONDER AND MAGNIFICENCE OF THESE STARS. YOU CAN, IF YOU KEEP LOOKING UP!

"EXTREME" ASTRONOMY

GREETINGS, GREETINGS, FELLOW STAR-GAZERS! WANT TO EXPERIENCE SOME "EXTREME" ASTRONOMY? WELL, GRAB YOUR PARACHUTE AND FOLLOW ME.

ON EARLY APRIL EVENINGS, THE BIG DIPPER IS POSITIONED SO THAT ITS WATER POURS OUT OF THE BOWL ONTO THE GROUND—A KIND OF CELESTIAL METAPHOR FOR "APRIL SHOWERS BRING MAY FLOWERS".

WELL, NOW'S A GREAT TIME ALSO TO SHOW YOU AN OLD TRICK I'VE LEARNED ABOUT USING THE HANDLE OF THE BIG DIPPER TO FIND OTHER VERY FAMOUS OBJECTS IN THE HEAVENS.

ARCTURUS

SPICA

SIMPLY FOLLOW A LINE THROUGH THE CURVING HANDLE OF THE DIPPER, THEN EXTEND THE CURVE AND ARC TO THE BRIGHT ORANGE-RED STAR, ARCTURUS.

"EXTREME" CLOSE UP

ARCTURUS

ARCTURUS IS THE 4TH BRIGHTEST STAR IN THE NIGHT SKY AND IS 37 LIGHT-YEARS DISTANT. THIS MAGNIFICENT TOPAZ ORB IS ZIPPING THROUGH SPACE AT ABOUT 87 MILES PER SECOND IN THE DIRECTION OF VIRGO, THE VIRGIN.

VROOOM!

AND THAT'S WHERE WE'LL FIND OUR NEXT TARGET, SPICA! ALL WE HAVE TO DO IS CONTINUE THAT GENTLE ARCING LINE AND "SPEED" ON TO SPICA, THE BRIGHTEST STAR IN VIRGO.

SPICA

SPICA IS MUCH FARTHER AWAY THAN ARCTURUS. IT LIES 260 LIGHT-YEARS DISTANT. BUT SPICA APPEARS ALMOST AS BRIGHT. WHY?

ARCTURUS

SPICA

SPICA IS A WHITE-HOT STAR AND IT BURNS 2,000 TIMES MORE INTENSELY THAN OUR SUN. WHEN YOU LOOK UP AT THE NIGHT SKY, APPEARANCES CAN BE VERY DECEIVING. IMAGINE TWO FLASHLIGHTS IN THE NIGHT.

SPICA

ONE FLASHLIGHT IS CLOSE TO YOU, BUT HAS WEAK BATTERIES. A MORE POWERFUL FLASHLIGHT IS FARTHER AWAY WITH FRESH BATTERIES. WELL, THE FLASHLIGHTS CAN APPEAR THE SAME BRIGHTNESS EVEN THOUGH THEY ARE AT DIFFERENT DISTANCES. THE WEAKER ONE WILL EVEN APPEAR MORE YELLOW (LIKE ARCTURUS).

AS

SO GO OUTSIDE, ARC TO ARCTURUS, AND SPEED ON TO SPICA. AND REMEMBER TO KEEP LOOKING UP!

ZOOM!

HARRINGTON

SUMMER

THE SUMMER TRIANGLE

THE MOST FAMOUS STAR PATTERN OF SUMMER IS THE SUMMER TRIANGLE. IT RISES IN THE EAST JUST AFTER SUNSET, WHEN SUMMER BEGINS.

ZENITH

AND IF YOU WAIT A FEW HOURS UNTIL MIDNIGHT, IT WILL BE ALMOST OVERHEAD AT THE ZENITH.

THE NAMES OF THE STARS ARE **VEGA**, **DENEB**, AND **ALTAIR**. TOGETHER, THEY MAKE UP THE **SUMMER TRIANGLE**.

VEGA

SUMMER TRIANGLE

DENEB

ALTAIR

BUT THE SUMMER TRIANGLE IS **NOT** A CONSTELLATION—IT'S AN **ASTERISM**, OR FAMILIAR GROUPING OF STARS.

CONSTELLATION

ASTERISM

YOU SEE, **VEGA**, THE BRIGHTEST STAR OF THE TRIANGLE, ACTUALLY BELONGS TO THE CONSTELLATION **LYRA**, THE LYRE, A SMALL HARP USED BY ANCIENT GREEK POETS.

VEGA

ALTAIR IS IN THE CONSTELLATION **AQUILA**, THE EAGLE, AND MARKS THE BIRD'S BRIGHT EYE.

ALTAIR

GO EAGLES!

AND **DENEB** MARKS THE TAIL OF THE CONSTELLATION CYGNUS, THE SWAN.

DENEB

YAY!

AND THESE THREE STARS ARE ABSOLUTELY FASCINATING!

THE BRIGHTEST OF THE THREE, VEGA, WAS THE FIRST STAR EVER TO BE PHOTOGRAPHED, WAY BACK IN 1850.

IT IS 2½ TIMES THE WIDTH OF OUR SUN, 54 TIMES BRIGHTER, AND 25 LIGHT-YEARS AWAY.

2½ TIMES WIDER, 54 TIMES BRIGHTER, AND 25 LIGHT-YEARS AWAY

VEGA SUN

TAP TAP
Z

ALTAIR IS ALMOST TWICE AS CLOSE, ONLY 17 LIGHT-YEARS AWAY. SO WHY ISN'T IT AS BRIGHT AS VEGA?

BOP!

SIMPLE. IT'S ONLY ABOUT 1½ TIMES OUR SUN'S DIAMETER AND ONLY 9 TIMES BRIGHTER. AND ALTAIR IS SUPER-WEIRD!

ALTAIR IS 17 LIGHT-YEARS AWAY

VEGA SUN ALTAIR

HOO HOO HA!

IT'S ONE OF THE FASTEST ROTATING STARS KNOWN.

ALTAIR RULES

DEN IS BES

IT SPINS AT 130 MILES PER SECOND AT ITS EQUATOR. THAT'S SO FAST THAT IT MAKES ALTAIR BULGE IN THE MIDDLE.

COOL!

IN FACT, ALTAIR IS TWICE AS WIDE FROM SIDE TO SIDE AS IT IS FROM TOP TO BOTTOM. BUT DENEB IS THE ALL-AROUND WINNER!

MR. HORKHEIMER

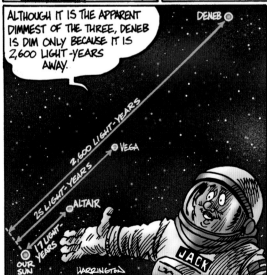

ALTHOUGH IT IS THE APPARENT DIMMEST OF THE THREE, DENEB IS DIM ONLY BECAUSE IT IS 2,600 LIGHT-YEARS AWAY.

DENEB

2,600 LIGHT-YEARS VEGA

25 LIGHT-YEARS ALTAIR

17 LIGHT-YEARS

OUR SUN

JACK

HARRINGTON

IN FACT, DENEB IS A WHOPPING 200 TIMES WIDER THAN OUR SUN AND 160,000 TIMES BRIGHTER!

200 TIMES WIDER

SUN DENEB

160,000 TIMES BRIGHTER!

SO, CATCH THESE THREE STARS AS THEY RISE IN THE EAST IN EARLY SUMMER, OR WAIT UNTIL MIDNIGHT WHEN THEY'RE OVERHEAD.

VEGA
DENEB
ALTAIR

VEGA
DENEB ALTAIR

THE MYSTERY OF JOB'S COFFIN

GREETINGS, **GREETINGS**, FELLOW STARGAZERS! YOU KNOW THE NIGHT SKY IS FULL OF MYSTERIES...

WELL, ONE OF THE **BIGGEST** MYSTERIES IS CENTERED ON ONE OF THE SMALLEST CONSTELLATIONS: DELPHINUS, THE DOLPHIN.

DELPHINUS

POOF!

DELPHINUS ALWAYS FOLLOWS THE SUMMER TRIANGLE ACROSS THE SKY. SO JUST LOOK TO THE EAST OF ALTAIR FOR A DIAMOND-SHAPED GROUPING OF STARS.

THAT'S THE DOLPHIN'S BODY. ITS TAIL IS MARKED BY A STAR A LITTLE TO THE SOUTH AND WEST.

IN GREEK MYTHOLOGY, THIS DOLPHIN PERSUADED THE SEA NYMPH AMPHITRITE TO MARRY POSEIDON, (NEPTUNE), RULER OF THE SEAS.

FOOMP!

JUST MARRIED

BUT THE TINY DIAMOND-SHAPED GROUPING OF STARS HAS ANOTHER, MYSTERIOUS INTERPRETATION. IN ENGLAND IT WAS KNOWN TO SOME AS JOB'S COFFIN.

THE PROBLEM IS THAT NO ONE KNOWS FOR CERTAIN, WHY.

THERE WAS ANOTHER MYSTERY. PEOPLE WONDERED WHY DELPHINUS' 2 BRIGHTEST STARS HAVE STRANGE NAMES — SUALOCIN AND **ROTANEV**.

WELL, IT TURNS OUT THAT SPELLED BACKWARD THEY'RE THE NAME OF AN ASTRONOMER'S ASSISTANT!

NICOLAUS VENATOR

AT LEAST **THAT** MYSTERY IS SOLVED.

THE RIVAL OF MARS AND HOW THE SCORPION LOST ITS CLAWS

LOOK SOUTH IN THE EARLY EVENING ON ANY SUMMER NIGHT, AND YOU'LL SEE A GIANT CONSTELLATION THAT LOOKS LIKE A FISH HOOK...

...OR THE CAPITAL LETTER J, WHICH DOES NOT STAND FOR JACK.

IT'S MY FAVORITE SUMMER CONSTELLATION, AND IT ACTUALLY LOOKS LIKE ITS NAME· SCORPIUS, THE SCORPION.

THE STAR THAT MARKS ITS HEART, ANTARES, IS RED. ANTARES MEANS "RIVAL OF MARS."

ANTARES
MARS

IT WAS SO NAMED BY OUR ANCESTORS BECAUSE WHENEVER MARS MOVES CLOSE TO ANTARES, THEY LOOK ALIKE.

YIPE!

BUT THIS IS AN ILLUSION. IN FACT, WE COULD LINE UP 130,000 RED PLANETS, SIDE BY SIDE, ACROSS THE MIDDLE OF ANTARES.

ANTARES

RUSH PROCESSING 130,000 COPIES MARS

HARRINGTON

INDEED, ANTARES IS 600 TIMES THE DIAMETER OF OUR SUN, AND 200 MILLION OF OUR SUNS WOULD FIT INSIDE IT.

ANTARES

IF WE COULD PLACE ONE EDGE OF ANTARES WHERE OUR SUN IS, ITS OPPOSITE EDGE WOULD EXTEND BEYOND JUPITER!

SUN
MERCURY
VENUS EARTH MARS
JUPITER

BUT SCORPIUS WAS AN EVEN **BIGGER** CONSTELLATION 2,000 YEARS AGO UNTIL THE ROMAN RULER JULIUS CAESAR DECIDED TO CHOP OFF ITS CLAWS.

HAIL   CAESAR

CAESAR RENAMED THE CLAWS LIBRA, FOR THE ROMAN SCALES OF JUSTICE. HOW UNJUST! BUT, JUST THE SAME, REMEMBER TO **KEEP LOOKING UP!**

SCORPION CLAWS

SPECIAL! FRESH SCORPION CLAWS!
WAS: NOW ONLY
MCMV   MCMIII

KITTY IN THE COSMOS AND TWO COMETS THAT NEVER WERE

GREETINGS, GREETINGS, FELLOW STARGAZERS. ALTHOUGH THERE ARE 88 OFFICIAL CONSTELLATIONS, NOT ONE OF THEM IS NAMED FOR A PUSSYCAT.

BUT, IF YOU KNOW WHERE TO LOOK, YOU CAN FIND TWO CAT'S EYES IN THE SUMMER SKY.

IN FACT, THE TWO STARS THAT MARK THE SCORPION'S STINGER ARE ALSO KNOWN AS THE CAT'S EYES.

SHAULA, THE BRIGHTER EYE, IS 11 TIMES THE SIZE OF OUR SUN AND 700 LIGHT-YEARS AWAY.

LESATH IS ONLY 520 LIGHT-YEARS AWAY.

YEON!

IN FACT, IT IS 7.5 TIMES THE SIZE OF OUR SUN AND 12,000 TIMES BRIGHTER. SOME PUSSYCAT, EH, FOLKS?

IF YOU LOOK ABOVE AND TO THE LEFT OF SHAULA AND LESATH, YOU'LL SEE TWO FAINT OBJECTS THAT LOOK LIKE COMETS... BUT THEY'RE NOT.

THE ONE CLOSEST TO THE STINGER, CALLED M7, IS A CLUSTER OF 80 STARS 800 LIGHT-YEARS AWAY.

M6, ALSO CALLED THE BUTTERFLY, HAS ABOUT 80 STARS TOO, BUT IS EXACTLY TWICE AS FAR AWAY— 1,600 LIGHT-YEARS.

EARTH
1,600 LIGHT-YEARS

M7 BYPASS
800 LIGHT-YEARS

I JUST LOVE THE STARS OF SUMMER. YOU'LL SEE THEM IF YOU KEEP LOOKING UP!

HARRINGTON

NAMED FOR A MYTHICAL CREATURE HALF MAN AND HALF HORSE, SAGITTARIUS FOLLOWS THE SCORPION ACROSS THE SKY.

HE IS AN ARCHER... AND A SHARPSHOOTER WITH A BOW AND ARROW.

AND THE TIP OF HIS ARROW POINTS TO THE MIDDLE OF THE WIDEST PART OF THE MILKY WAY.

POINK

IN FACT, HIS ARROW POINTS AT THE VERY CENTER OF OUR HUGE FAMILY OF STARS, THE MILKY WAY GALAXY, ABOUT 30,000 LIGHT-YEARS AWAY.

YOU SEE, OUR SUN IS ABOUT TWO-THIRDS OF THE WAY OUT FROM THE MILKY WAY'S CENTER.

GALAXY CENTER

SAGITTARIUS

SUN

SCORPIUS

THE MILKY WAY APPEARS TO BULGE BETWEEN SAGITTARIUS AND SCORPIUS BECAUSE THE HUB OF OUR GALAXY IS IN THIS DIRECTION.

SAGITTARIUS

SCORPIUS

SAGITTARIUS ALSO CONTAINS ONE OF MY FAVORITE ASTERISMS, THE TEAPOT. BY THE WAY, AN ASTERISM IS A CLUSTER OF STARS SMALLER THAN A CONSTELLATION.

AND TOWARD THE END OF SUMMER, AS SCORPIUS SETS IN THE SOUTHWEST...

SOUTH WEST

THE TEAPOT IS TILTED SO THAT IT LOOKS LIKE IT'S POURING TEA ON THE SCORPION'S TAIL. POOR SCORPIUS!

FIRST, THE ROMANS CHOPPED OFF THE SCORPION'S CLAWS TO CREATE THE CONSTELLATION LIBRA, AND NOW WE POUR TEA ON ITS TAIL! IT'S ALWAYS EXCITING WHEN WE KEEP LOOKING UP!

TWANG

SORRY, LITTLE FELLOW...

A WEEK OF DUE-EAST SUNRISES AND DUE-WEST SUNSETS

GREETINGS, GREETINGS, FELLOW STARGAZERS. IT'S SEPTEMBER, SO GET READY FOR SOME IN-YOUR-FACE SUNRISES...

AND IN-YOUR-FACE SUNSETS!

EVERY YEAR ON THE FIRST DAY OF FALL, WE CELEBRATE WHAT ASTRONOMERS CALL THE AUTUMNAL EQUINOX. AND ON THE FIRST DAY OF SPRING, WE REJOICE IN WHAT ASTRONOMERS CALL THE VERNAL EQUINOX.

FALL

SPRING

ONLY AT THESE TIMES OF THE YEAR DOES THE SUN RISE DIRECTLY DUE EAST AND SET DUE WEST. IF YOU'RE GOING TO SCHOOL ON A DUE-EAST ROAD AFTER SUNRISE, THE SUN WILL BE DIRECTLY OVER THE YELLOW LINE IN THE MIDDLE OF THE ROAD.

IF YOU GET A RIDE HOME AFTER PLAYING OUTSIDE AT SUNSET, AND ARE ON A DUE-WEST HIGHWAY, THE SUN WILL SET DIRECTLY OVER THE YELLOW LINE IN THE MIDDLE OF THE ROAD.

BUT WHAT **ARE** THE EQUINOXES, ANYWAY?

WELL, THE WORD EQUINOX COMES FROM THE LATIN "EQUI," WHICH MEANS EQUAL, AND "NOX," WHICH MEANS NIGHT.

=

NIGHT

ON THE TWO DAYS OF THE EQUINOXES THE HOURS OF NIGHT ARE EQUAL TO THE HOURS OF DAYLIGHT. ONE EQUINOX MARKS THE FIRST DAY OF SPRING, AND THE OTHER ONE MARKS THE FIRST DAY OF AUTUMN.

SPRING

MOON

SUN

AUTUMN

SO BE SURE TO PUT THOSE SUN VISORS DOWN AS YOU GO BACK AND FORTH TO SCHOOL ON THESE TWO DAYS. AND DON'T FORGET TO KEEP LOOKING UP!

HARRINGTON

HOW TO FIND THE "FALSE DAWN" OF OMAR KHAYYÁM

GREETINGS, GREETINGS, FELLOW STARGAZERS. THE NIGHT SKY IS ROMANTIC.

ALMOST 1,000 YEARS AGO, OMAR KHAYYÁM OF PERSIA MADE A POETIC ALLUSION TO A "FALSE DAWN."

WELL, THE "FALSE DAWN" IS NOT JUST POETRY. IT'S REAL!

IF WE COULD GO FAR INTO SPACE AND LOOK BACK DOWN ON OUR SOLAR SYSTEM WITH SUPER-HUMAN VISION...

WE WOULD NOTICE A VAST, FAINT -ALMOST IMPERCEPTIBLE- CLOUD EXTENDING OUTWARD FROM THE SUN IN THE PLANE OF THE ORBITS OF MERCURY, VENUS, EARTH, AND SLIGHTLY BEYOND.

THE CLOUD IS MADE UP OF TRILLIONS AND TRILLIONS OF COSMIC DUST PARTICLES, WHICH SCATTER SUNLIGHT, MAKING THEM VISIBLE.

IN SEPTEMBER, THAT CLOUD IS ALMOST VERTICAL TO THE HORIZON FROM OUR POINT OF VIEW, SO IT'S A GOOD TIME TO SEE OMAR KHAYYÁM'S "FALSE DAWN."

LOOK FOR A VERY FAINT PYRAMID OF LIGHT IN THE EAST ABOUT TWO HOURS BEFORE THE REAL DAWN.

TO SEE IT, YOU MUST BE FAR AWAY FROM CITY LIGHTS AND OUTSIDE WHEN THERE IS NO MOONLIGHT.

THE SCIENTIFIC NAME OF THIS PHENOMENON IS THE "ZODIACAL LIGHT," BECAUSE THE CLOUD RUNS THROUGH THE CONSTELLATIONS OF THE ZODIAC.

ONCE YOU'VE FOUND IT, I THINK YOU'LL KNOW WHY IT APPEARED IN POETRY CENTURIES BEFORE IT APPEARED IN SCIENTIFIC WRITINGS. I'M JACK HORKHEIMER, KEEP LOOKING UP!

 STARS FOR AN INDIAN SUMMER

GREETINGS, GREETINGS, FELLOW STARGAZERS! THIS IS THAT TIME OF YEAR WHEN ACROSS THE MIDDLE AND NORTHERN LATITUDES OF THE UNITED STATES, A STRANGE AND WONDERFUL PHENOMENON OCCURS.

YOU SEE, EVEN THOUGH THE DAYS AND NIGHTS HAVE BEEN GETTING CHILLIER AND CHILLIER, SUDDENLY, A FEW UNSEASON-ABLY WARM, GOLDEN DAYS OCCUR- CALLED INDIAN SUMMER,

WHEN I WAS A KID LIVING IN WISCONSIN, WE ALWAYS LOOKED FORWARD TO THIS LAST ECHO OF SUMMER, WHICH ALWAYS SEEMED TO BE A MINIATURE SEASON OUT OF TIME AND PLACE. INDEED, INDIAN SUMMER ALWAYS SEEMED LIKE SUMMER'S LAST HURRAH!

AND JUST AS SUMMER SEEMS TO HAVE A DIFFICULT TIME LEAVING, SO TOO DO SOME OF THE STARS THAT DOMINATED SUMMER NIGHTS. LET ME SHOW YOU MY FAVORITE!

WHAP!

IF YOU GO OUT AN HOUR AFTER SUNSET AND LOOK ALMOST DIRECTLY OVERHEAD, THE MOST BRILLIANT STAR YOU'LL SEE IS VEGA, WHICH BELONGS TO THE TINY CONSTELLATION LYRA, THE HARP, AND IS AT THE APEX OF THE SUMMER TRIANGLE.

VEGA

VEGA IS THE 5TH BRIGHTEST STAR WE CAN SEE FROM EARTH. IT GLISTENS A CRISP, SHARP, BLUE-WHITE, WHICH TELLS US THAT IT IS A MUCH, MUCH HOTTER STAR THAN OUR OWN YELLOW-ORANGE SUN.

10,000°C   5,500°C

WHAT I REALLY LIKE TO THINK ABOUT WHEN I GAZE UP AT VEGA IS THAT OUR SUN IS RACING HEAD-ON TOWARD VEGA AT THE INCREDIBLE SPEED OF 68,000 KILOMETERS PER HOUR. EVEN THOUGH VEGA'S DISTANCE IS ONLY 25 LIGHT-YEARS AWAY, AT THIS SPEED IT WOULD TAKE OUR SUN ALMOST A HALF BILLION YEARS TO REACH IT, IF VEGA WASN'T ALSO MOVING.

VEGA

VEGA OR BUST!

ASTRONOMERS CALL THIS POINT IN SPACE TOWARD WHICH OUR SUN IS RUSHING "THE APEX OF THE SUN'S WAY." SO, DURING INDIAN SUMMER, LOOK TO VEGA AND LET YOUR SPIRIT SOAR, YOU MIGHT FEEL OUR TINY EARTH HURTLING THROUGH SPACE TOWARD IT. WHAT A WONDERFUL ADVENTURE AWAITS YOU, IF YOU KEEP LOOKING UP!

APEX OF THE SUN'S WAY

RICH HARRINGTON

THE SUMMER TRIANGLE GIVES WAY TO THE AUTUMN SQUARE

GREETINGS, GREETINGS, FELLOW STARGAZERS!

DID YOU KNOW THAT WHEN THE SEASONS CHANGE ON EARTH, SO TOO DO THE STARS CHANGE OVERHEAD? EVER HEAR OF THE PHRASE "THE STARS OF THE SEASON"?

CHOP!

"STARS OF THE SEASON" USUALLY REFERS TO THE MAJOR STARS AND STAR GROUPS THAT REACH THEIR HIGHEST POSITION ABOVE THE HORIZON IN MID EVENING DURING A SPECIFIC SEASON.

BYE! SO LONG! BYE! WEST

IF YOU GO OUTSIDE THIS AUTUMN AND LOOK JUST WEST OF OVERHEAD IN THE FIRST WEEK OF OCTOBER, YOU WILL SEE THREE BRIGHT STARS. THESE MAKE UP THE POINTS OF THE SUMMER TRIANGLE.

VEGA
DENEB
ALTAIR
CHOK!

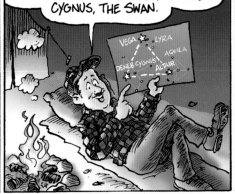

THE BRIGHTEST STAR IS VEGA, IN THE CONSTELLATION LYRA, THE HARP; THE SECOND BRIGHTEST IS ALTAIR IN AQUILA, THE EAGLE; AND THE THIRD BRIGHTEST IS DENEB IN CYGNUS, THE SWAN.

VEGA LYRA
AQUILA
DENEB CYGNUS ALTAIR

NOW THAT IT IS AUTUMN, THESE THREE BRILLIANT STARS OF SUMMER ARE BEGINNING THEIR SLOW DESCENT TOWARD THE WESTERN HORIZON.

NORTH EAST SOUTH WEST

SO LONG, PAL!

BYE! SEE YA!

AND REPLACING THEM ALMOST OVERHEAD ARE THE FOUR MUCH DIMMER STARS THAT MAKE UP THE AUTUMN SQUARE — THE GREAT SQUARE OF PEGASUS.

SCHEAT PEGASUS
ANDROMEDA
ALPHERATZ MARKAB
ALGENIB

THE ANCIENT BABYLONIANS SAID THE AUTUMN SQUARE WAS "THE DOORWAY TO PARADISE." HOW POETIC!

WITH ITS COLORFUL LEAVES IN MANY PARTS OF THE UNITED STATES AND ITS BOUNTY OF CROPS, AUTUMN DOES SEEM TO BE A VISUAL PARADISE ON EARTH. HOW APPROPRIATE THAT THIS LOVELY COSMIC SQUARE HERALDS THE SEASON. I'M JACK HORKHEIMER— KEEP LOOKING UP!

HARRIK '93

THE MILKY WAY AT ITS VERY BEST

Panel 1: GREETINGS, GREETINGS, FELLOW STARGAZERS! EVERY OCTOBER, THE MILKY WAY IS AT ITS BEST FOR VIEWING - RIGHT AFTER SUNSET.

Panel 2: IF IT'S REALLY CLEAR OUT, AND YOU'RE FAR FROM CITY LIGHTS, THE MILKY WAY WILL LOOK LIKE A FAINT RIBBON OF LIGHT.

Panel 3: THE MILKY WAY STRETCHES UPWARD FROM THE NORTHERN HORIZON, THROUGH CASSIOPEIA AND THE SUMMER TRIANGLE, THEN PAST THE ZENITH DOWN TO THE SOUTHERN HORIZON, THROUGH THE TEAPOT OF SAGITTARIUS AND THE TAIL OF THE SCORPION.

ZENITH · SAGITTARIUS · CASSIOPEIA · SCORPIO · NORTH · SOUTH

Panel 4: YEARS AGO, THE MILKY WAY COULD EASILY BE SEEN FROM ALMOST ANYWHERE, BUT TODAY CITY LIGHTS OFTEN WASH IT FROM VIEW.

NOW PLAYI CATS

Panel 5: THERE IS SO MUCH ARTIFICIAL LIGHTING TODAY THAT ASTRONOMERS REFER TO IT AS "LIGHT POLLUTION." IN FACT, SO MUCH OF THE NIGHT SKY IS WASHED FROM VIEW BY IT THAT MOST PEOPLE HAVE NEVER EVEN SEEN THE MILKY WAY.

Panel 6: KEEP IN MIND THAT THE MILKY WAY IS NOT A COSMIC CLOUD, BUT THE COMBINED LIGHT OF BILLIONS OF STARS SO FAR AWAY THAT THEIR LIGHT FUZZES TOGETHER IN A BLUR.

MILKY WAY REVEALE

Panel 7: IN FACT, IF YOU LOOK THROUGH A PAIR OF BINOCULARS OR A TELESCOPE ANYWHERE ALONG THE MILKY WAY, YOU WILL SEE WHAT LOOKS LIKE MILLIONS OF PIN POINTS OF LIGHT, EACH BEING A STAR LIKE OUR OWN SUN.

Panel 8: FEEL INSIGNIFICANT? YOU MIGHT, IF YOU KEEP LOOKING UP!

HARRINGTON

The MYSTERY of the Seven Sisters

GREETINGS, GREETINGS, FELLOW STARGAZERS. WE CELEBRATE HALLOWEEN THIS MONTH, SO HERE'S A LITTLE MYSTERY FOR YOU.

GO OUTSIDE AROUND 8 O'CLOCK P.M. AND LOOK TOWARD THE EAST. YOU SHOULD SEE A SHIMMERING LITTLE CLUSTER OF STELLAR GRAPES. THOSE ARE THE PLEIADES, OR SEVEN SISTERS.

MY FAVORITE DESCRIPTION OF THEM COMES FROM THE 19TH CENTURY POET LORD TENNYSON, WHO SAID:

"MANY A NIGHT I SAW THE PLEIADS RISING THROUGH THE MELLOW SHADE, GLIMMER LIKE A SWARM OF FIREFLIES, TANGLED IN A SILVER BRAID..."

NOW, FOR THE MYSTERY. APPARENTLY, ONE OF THE SEVEN SISTERS IS LOST! MYTH TELLERS FROM THE EARLY GREEKS TO THE PRIMITIVE HEADHUNTERS OF BORNEO HAVE LAMENTED THE STAR'S SUDDEN DISAPPEARANCE.

TODAY, MANY PEOPLE STILL SEE ONLY SIX BRIGHT STARS IN THE PLEIADES WITH THEIR UNAIDED EYES.

SEVEN! SEVEN! SIX! SIX! SEVEN! SIX! SIX!

IF WE USE BINOCULARS OR A TELESCOPE TO FIND THE MISSING SISTER, WE GET ANOTHER SURPRISE. THERE ARE **HUNDREDS** OF STARS (NOT SIX OR SEVEN) IN THE PLEIADES. IT'S A TRUE STAR CLUSTER SWIMMING IN GAS! **WOW!**

COULD THE MYSTERIOUS SEVENTH SISTER HAVE FADED TO BECOME ONE OF THE HUNDREDS OF FAINTER STARS IN THE CLUSTER? IF SO, WHICH ONE IS IT?

HMMMM...

THE FACT IS, THERE'S NO WAY TO KNOW FOR SURE. BUT YOU CAN EASILY DETERMINE THE NUMBER OF STARS **YOU** SEE IN THE PLEIADES. TO FIND OUT, JUST KEEP LOOKING UP!

THE FARTHEST THING YOU CAN SEE WITH THE NAKED EYE

GREETINGS, GREETINGS, FELLOW STARGAZERS! HAVE YOU EVER WONDERED ABOUT THIS...?

WELL, DON'T BE FOOLED, BECAUSE EVEN WITH THE NAKED EYE YOU CAN SEE 10 MILES AWAY, AND EVEN FARTHER!

WE CAN SEE THE MOON, AND IT'S 250,000 MILES AWAY. AND THE SUN IS 93 MILLION MILES AWAY!

ALPHA CENTAURI IS 4.4 LIGHT-YEARS AWAY. SINCE THERE ARE 6 TRILLION MILES IN ONE LIGHT-YEAR, WE'RE SEEING A STAR THAT IS 26 TRILLION MILES AWAY!

← ALPHA CENTAURI

STAR AHOY, CAP'N!

ARR... SHE LOOKS ABOUT 26 TRILLION MILES AWAY!

SS STARGAZER★

NOW, ON AUTUMN NIGHTS, CASSIOPEIA LIES ABOVE THE NORTH STAR, AND ABOVE IT IS THE GREAT SQUARE OF PEGASUS, THE HORSE.

PEGASUS HAS TWO HIND LEGS THAT DOUBLE AS THE CONSTELLATION ANDROMEDA.

ANDROMEDA

ON A CLEAR MOONLESS NIGHT, YOU CAN SEE A FUZZY CLOUD IN ANDROMEDA. IT LOOKS EVEN BETTER THROUGH A PAIR OF BINOCULARS.

BUT THIS FUZZY DIM CLOUD IS, IN FACT, A GIGANTIC GALAXY OF PERHAPS 300 BILLION STARS, 2½ MILLION LIGHT-YEARS AWAY!

ANDROMEDA

MILKY WAY

HOW MANY MILES IS THAT? SIMPLY MULTIPLY 6 TRILLION MILES BY 2.5 MILLION.

6,000,000,000,000 × 2,500,000

WINK!

REMEMBER, WHEN YOU LOOK AT THE ANDROMEDA GALAXY, YOU ARE SEEING IT AS IT APPEARED BEFORE HUMANS WALKED UPON THE EARTH. BUT YOU'LL SEE IT, IF ONLY YOU KEEP LOOKING UP!

SOME DIFFERENT BIRDS FOR THANKSGIVING

GREETINGS, GREETINGS, FELLOW STARGAZERS! IT'S THAT TIME OF YEAR WHEN MANY PEOPLE IN NORTH AMERICA HAVE A BIRD ON THE TABLE TO CELEBRATE THANKSGIVING.

BUT DID YOU KNOW THAT EVERY THANKSGIVING NIGHT THE SKY IS LOADED WITH BIRDS, TOO?

LOOK TOWARD THE WEST ANY CLEAR NIGHT DURING THANKSGIVING WEEK JUST AFTER SUNSET AND YOU'LL SEE THE THREE BRIGHT STARS MAKING UP THE SUMMER TRIANGLE. BUT THIS TIME OF YEAR I UNOFFICIALLY CALL IT THE POULTRY TRIANGLE.

YOU SEE, THE EASTERN STAR IS DENEB, IN CYGNUS, THE SWAN. THE WESTERN STAR IS ALTAIR, IN AQUILA, THE EAGLE, AND THE STAR CLOSEST TO THE NORTHWEST HORIZON IS VEGA, IN LYRA, THE HARP.

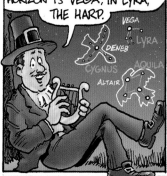

YES, I SAID, "THE HARP"...BUT LYRA WASN'T ALWAYS A HARP!

LONG BEFORE LYRA BECAME A HARP, IT WAS A COSMIC TURTLE!

BEFORE LYRA BECAME A COSMIC TURTLE IT WAS, YOU GUESSED IT, A **BIRD**! IN FACT, ANCIENT RECORDS TELL US THAT LYRA'S ASSOCIATION WITH A BIRD GOES BACK OVER 2,000 YEARS.

IN ANCIENT INDIA, LYRA WAS A HEAVENLY VULTURE. BABYLONIAN KINGS AND QUEENS SAW IT AS THEIR MYTHICAL STORM BIRD, URAKHGA. IN ANCIENT ARABIA, IT WAS THE SWOOPING EAGLE OF THE DESERT... OR A GOOSE. PERFECT FARE FOR ANYONE'S THANKSGIVING BANQUET!

LYRA

ANCIENT INDIA = VULTURE

ANCIENT ARABIA = EAGLE OR GOOSE

LYRA HAS ALSO SEEN OTHER FEATHERY INCARNATIONS. INDEED, IT WAS ONCE KNOWN AS A GREAT OSPREY, AND AT ANOTHER TIME AS A WOOD FALCON. IN FACT, AT THE TIME OF THE AMERICAN REVOLUTION, THESE STARS WERE DEPICTED AS AN EAGLE WITH A LYRE (OR HARP) IN ITS BEAK.

SO, THIS THANKSGIVING WEEK AFTER YOU'VE HAD YOUR TURKEY, WHY NOT GO OUTSIDE FOR SOME BIRDS OF A DIFFERENT FEATHER AND THANK HEAVEN YOU'LL NEVER GET ANY OF THEM AS LEFTOVERS. I'M JACK HORKHEIMER, HAPPY THANKSGIVING AND KEEP LOOKING UP!

METEOR WATCHING - IT'S EASY!

I'M GOING TO SHOW YOU HOW TO WATCH A METEOR SHOWER! AND AUTUMN HAS TWO GREAT ONES — THE LEONIDS (NOVEMBER 16-17) AND THE GEMINIDS (DECEMBER 12-13).

METEOR SHOWERS ARE ALWAYS BEST AFTER MIDNIGHT, SO HERE'S THE HARD PART... SET YOUR ALARM— AND GET UP WHEN IT RINGS!

NOV. 16

BRINNNGG!!

NEXT, BE SURE TO DRESS WARMLY. MAYBE MAKE SOME HOT CHOCOLATE AND PUT IT IN A THERMOS!

NOW, GO OUTSIDE AND SET UP A RECLINING LAWN CHAIR. LIE ON IT WITH A PILLOW BEHIND YOUR HEAD AND WRAP UP IN A BLANKET. TURN ON YOUR FAVORITE RADIO STATION AND POUR SOME HOT CHOCOLATE.

STRANGERS IN THE NIGHT...

AND FINALLY, LOOK UP (IT DOESN'T MATTER WHERE YOU LOOK) AND WAIT FOR METEORS TO STREAK ACROSS THE SKY. EASY!

YOU MAY SEE ABOUT ONE METEOR PER MINUTE. BUT, IF WE HAVE A METEOR STORM— WELL, *THAT* WOULD BE SPECTACULAR. BUT THERE'S ONLY ONE WAY TO FIND OUT... YOU HAVE TO KEEP LOOKING UP!

GREETINGS, GREETINGS, FELLOW STARGAZERS! DID YOU KNOW THAT METEORS IN A METEOR SHOWER APPEAR TO RAIN DOWN FROM A SINGLE POINT IN THE SKY?

THAT'S RIGHT! ASTRONOMERS CALL THAT POINT THE "RADIANT", AND IT'S A VISUAL PUZZLE!

RADIANT

OOF! MESSY COMET!

AS THE EARTH ORBITS THE SUN, IT PERIODICALLY PASSES THROUGH STREAMS OF PARTICLES LEFT BY COMETS. WHEN THE EARTH'S ATMOSPHERE AND THE PARTICLES COLLIDE...

WE SEE A METEOR SHOWER!

NOW FOR THE PUZZLE!

THE METEORS ENTERING EARTH'S ATMOSPHERE ALL TRAVEL IN PARALLEL PATHS. SINCE TWO PARALLEL PATHS CANNOT INTERSECT, HOW CAN METEORS MEET AT A RADIANT?

SIMPLE! THEY DON'T! IT JUST LOOKS THAT WAY! VIEWING A RADIANT IS NO DIFFERENT THAN SEEING THE TWO SIDES OF A STRAIGHT ROAD MEETING ON THE DISTANT HORIZON. IT'S JUST A MATTER OF "PERSPECTIVE"

RICH HARRINGTON

WHEN YOU KEEP LOOKING UP!

WHY THE WINTER SOLSTICE WAS A TIME OF FEAR

GREETINGS, GREETINGS, FELLOW STARGAZERS. I KNOW A LOT OF US FEAR THE NIGHT. THAT'S EASY TO UNDERSTAND. BUT THE WINTER SOLSTICE?

WELL, TWO THOUSAND YEARS AGO, THE WINTER SOLSTICE WAS ALMOST UNIVERSALLY FEARED BECAUSE MANY PEOPLE BELIEVED THAT ON THAT DAY THE WORLD MIGHT COME TO AN END.

THE WORLD WILL END TODAY.

TODAY IS THE END OF THE WORLD.

THIS IS IT.

YOU SEE, THEY WERE SKYWATCHERS. SO THEY KNEW THAT ON THE FIRST DAY OF SPRING, THE VERNAL EQUINOX, THE SUN RISES EXACTLY DUE EAST AND SETS DUE WEST.

EAST

WEST

THE SUN THEN MOVES SLOWLY NORTHWARD, UNTIL THE FIRST DAY OF SUMMER, THE SUMMER SOLSTICE. THAT'S WHEN THE SUN SEEMS TO STAND STILL FOR A COUPLE OF DAYS. IN FACT, "SOLSTICE" LITERALLY MEANS THE SUN (SOL) STANDS STILL (STICE).

OVER THE NEXT SIX MONTHS, THE SUN WOULD MOVE SLOWLY SOUTH. BY THE 3RD WEEK OF DECEMBER, THE WINTER SOLSTICE, IT WOULD ONCE AGAIN STAND STILL FOR A COUPLE OF DAYS.

SOUTH

NOW, MANY ANCIENT PEOPLE BELIEVED THAT THE SUN MADE THIS JOURNEY BETWEEN SUMMER AND WINTER (NORTH AND SOUTH) BECAUSE IT WAS A GOD AND HAD A WILL OF ITS OWN.

I'M OUTTA HERE...

SOUTH

OUR ANCESTORS BELIEVED THAT IF THEY DID NOT PRAY TO THE SUN EVERY THIRD WEEK OF DECEMBER THE SUN JUST MIGHT CONTINUE ITS JOURNEY SOUTH UNTIL EARTH WAS PLUNGED INTO ETERNAL COLDNESS AND NIGHT!

PLEASE COME BACK!!

BRRRR!

OF COURSE, EVERY DECEMBER THEIR PRAYERS WORKED. THE SUN WOULD STAND STILL, SO TO SPEAK, AND THEN BEGIN TO SLOWLY RETRACE ITS PATH NORTHWARD. YOU CAN RETRACE THIS PATH YOURSELF IF YOU KEEP LOOKING UP!

HARRINGTON

GREETINGS, GREETINGS, FELLOW STARGAZERS, AND YES, INDEED, YOU HEARD RIGHT. WINTER FOR THE NORTHERN HEMISPHERE IS THE SHORTEST SEASON OF THE ENTIRE YEAR.

NOT ONLY IS WINTER THE SHORTEST SEASON, IT'S GETTING EVEN SHORTER. WHY? LET ME SHOW YOU.

EVERYONE KNOWS THAT OUR EARTH MAKES ONE TRIP AROUND THE SUN ONCE A YEAR. MORE PRECISELY, THE TRIP TAKES 365¼ EARTH DAYS.

BUT ACCORDING TO KEPLER'S LAWS OF MOTION, THE CLOSER AN OBJECT TO THE SUN, THE FASTER IT WILL TRAVEL; THE FARTHER FROM THE SUN, THE SLOWER IT TRAVELS. AND THIS APPLIES TO OUR EARTH AS IT TRAVELS IN ITS ORBIT.

YOU SEE, OUR EARTH'S ORBIT IS NOT A PERFECT CIRCLE, BUT A SLIGHTLY STRETCHED OUT ONE CALLED AN ELLIPSE. AND THE SUN IS NOT AT THE CENTER OF THIS ELLIPSE. SO THE EARTH VARIES ITS DISTANCE FROM THE SUN DURING THE YEAR.

GA-GOING

BELIEVE IT OR NOT, THE EARTH IS CLOSEST TO THE SUN DURING THE FIRST WEEK OF EVERY JANUARY AND FARTHEST FROM THE SUN THE FIRST WEEK OF EVERY JULY. SO OUR EARTH TRAVELS MUCH FASTER WHEN IT'S WINTER IN THE NORTHERN HEMISPHERE AND MUCH MORE SLOWLY DURING THE SUMMER.

BRRRRR

IT TAKES 94 DAYS FOR THE EARTH TO TRAVEL FROM THE FIRST DAY OF SUMMER TO THE FIRST DAY OF AUTUMN, MAKING SUMMER THE LONGEST SEASON OF ALL. THE EARTH WHIPS THROUGH WINTER IN ONLY 89 DAYS.

94 DAYS

AUTUMN — SUMMER

WINTER — SPRING

89 DAYS

WHEN IT REACHES ITS CLOSEST POINT TO THE SUN DURING THE FIRST WEEK OF JANUARY, THE EARTH IS ZIPPING ALONG AT 67,307 MILES PER HOUR. THAT'S 2,187 MILES PER HOUR FASTER THAN IT TRAVELED IN JULY.

ZOOM!

BEEP!

67,307 MPH

AND WINTER WILL CONTINUE TO GET SHORTER UNTIL AROUND A.D. 3,500, WHEN WINTER WILL BE ONLY 88.71 DAYS LONG. SO IF ANYONE TELLS YOU WINTERS ARE GETTING LONGER, THEY'RE WRONG.

BUT IF WINTER IS STILL TOO LONG FOR YOU, TAKE COMFORT IN THE FACT THAT IF YOU LIVED ON PLUTO, WINTER IN THE NORTHERN HEMISPHERE WOULD TAKE 45 YEARS. WHICH WOULD MEAN THAT YOU'D REALLY HAVE TO BUNDLE UP AS YOU KEEP LOOKING UP!

CHIP CHIP

WELCOME TO PLUTO

NO PARKING

HARRINGTON

★ THE NEW YEAR'S EVE STAR: A STORY RETOLD ★★

GREETINGS, GREETINGS, FELLOW STARGAZERS! I'M GOING TO TELL YOU ABOUT SOMETHING THAT WILL HAPPEN EVERY NEW YEAR'S EVE FOR AS LONG AS THE WORLD GOES AROUND.

IT'S SOMETHING THAT TO ME IS ALMOST MAGICAL BECAUSE OF ITS SHEER COINCIDENCE.

YOU SEE, AT THE STROKE OF MIDNIGHT ON NEW YEAR'S EVE, THE BRIGHTEST STAR IN THE HEAVENS REACHES ITS HIGHEST POINT ABOVE THE HORIZON AND SHINES LIKE A DAZZLING BEACON, WELCOMING THE NEW YEAR.

TO PREPARE YOURSELF FOR THIS AMAZING EVENT, GO OUTSIDE AT 7 P.M. (YOUR LOCAL TIME) ON NEW YEAR'S EVE AND LOOK UP AT THE SKY. FACE DUE SOUTH AND DRAW AN IMAGINARY LINE FROM THE HORIZON STRAIGHT UP TO THE POINT DIRECTLY OVERHEAD, AND THEN DOWN THE OTHER SIDE OF THE SKY TO THE HORIZON DUE NORTH.

THAT IMAGINARY LINE IS CALLED A "MERIDIAN". SO, AS THE EARTH SLOWLY AND ENDLESSLY ROTATES ON ITS AXIS FROM WEST TO EAST, WE ARE TREATED NIGHTLY TO THE GRANDEST OPTICAL ILLUSION IN NATURE... THAT OF WATCHING THE STARS SEEM TO RISE IN THE EAST AND TRAVEL ACROSS THE SKY, EVENTUALLY SETTING IN THE WEST.

AND IF YOU WATCH CAREFULLY, YOU WILL REALIZE THAT THE HIGHEST POINT ANY STAR REACHES ABOVE THE HORIZON IN ITS NIGHTLY JOURNEY IS SMACK DAB ON THE MERIDIAN.

SEVERAL YEARS AGO, WHEN I WAS IN THE FIELD RESEARCHING WHICH PLANETS WOULD BE HIGH UP OFF THE HORIZON FOR VIEWING THAT NEW YEAR'S EVE, I STUMBLED ACROSS SOMETHING THAT WAS TO ME AN AMAZING COINCIDENCE. SOMETHING THAT I HAD NEVER READ ABOUT IN ANY ASTRONOMY BOOK.

AND THAT COINCIDENCE IS: NO MATTER WHERE YOU HAPPEN TO BE ON NEW YEAR'S EVE, AS HOUR AFTER HOUR PASSES, DRAWING CLOSER TO MIDNIGHT, THE BRIGHTEST STAR IN THE HEAVENS, SIRIUS, WILL SLOWLY CLIMB UP THE SOUTHEASTERN SKY AND AT MIDNIGHT REACH ITS HIGHEST POINT, AND BE ON THE MERIDIAN.

THINK OF IT... THE BRIGHTEST STAR VISIBLE FROM OUR PLANET REACHES ITS HIGHEST POINT ABOVE THE HORIZON AT MIDNIGHT EVERY YEAR ON NEW YEAR'S EVE! HOW WONDERFUL! HOW PERFECT! A COSMIC REMINDER THAT THIS BRIGHTEST OF STELLAR LIGHTS IS WELCOMING IN THE NEW YEAR, GIVING US ALL HOPE FOR A BRIGHT NEW BEGINNING.

IF YOU HAPPEN TO MISS THIS WONDROUS EVENT ON THIS NEW YEAR'S EVE, DON'T FRET. SIRIUS WILL BE IN ALMOST THE SAME SPOT AT MIDNIGHT EACH NIGHT FOR THE FIRST WEEK OF THE NEW YEAR, SO START YOUR NEW YEAR BRIGHT WITH COSMIC LIGHT. IT'S EASY, IF YOU KEEP LOOKING UP!

THE DAY THE EARTH NEARS THE SUN

GREETINGS, GREETINGS, FELLOW STARGAZERS. WOULD YOU BELIEVE THAT EVEN THOUGH IT'S WINTER THE EARTH IS CLOSER TO THE SUN IN JANUARY THAN IT IS DURING THE SUMMER IN JULY?

NORTH POLE

THAT'S RIGHT! EARTH IS ABOUT 94.5 MILLION MILES AWAY FROM THE SUN IN JULY. THEN, IN JUST SIX MONTHS TIME, IT CAREENS OVER 3.1 MILLION MILES CLOSER. ARE WE ON A COLLISION COURSE WITH THE SUN?

LOOK OUT!

NORTH POLE

3.1 MILLION MILES CLOSER

NO, NOT TO WORRY. YOU SEE, THIS HAPPENS EVERY YEAR, JUST LIKE CLOCKWORK. THE SIMPLE REASON IS THAT OUR EARTH'S ORBIT AROUND THE SUN IS NOT A PERFECT CIRCLE, BUT A SLIGHTLY STRETCHED OUT CIRCLE, CALLED AN ELLIPSE.

ELLIPSE

IT JUST SO HAPPENS THAT EVERY JANUARY OUR EARTH IS AT THAT POINT IN THE ELLIPSE CLOSEST TO THE SUN. EVERY JULY, IT IS AT THAT POINT FARTHEST FROM THE SUN. SO WHY IS IT COLDER IN JANUARY THAN IT IS IN JULY?

IT ISN'T IF YOU LIVE SOUTH OF THE EQUATOR, WHERE IT IS SUMMER INSTEAD OF WINTER IN JANUARY. WHY IS THIS THE CASE? BECAUSE OUR EARTH IS OUT OF KILTER, MEANING ITS AXIS IS TILTED 23½ DEGREES TO ITS ORBIT.

23½ DEGREES

RICH HARRINGTON

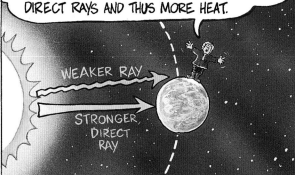

IN JANUARY, OUR NORTHERN HEMISPHERE IS TILTED FARTHER AWAY FROM THE SUN THAN THE SOUTHERN HEMISPHERE IS. SO IT GETS FEWER DIRECT RAYS FROM THE SUN AND THUS LESS HEAT. THE SOUTHERN HEMISPHERE, IN JANUARY, IS TILTED MORE TOWARD THE SUN, SO IT GETS MORE DIRECT RAYS AND THUS MORE HEAT.

WEAKER RAY

STRONGER, DIRECT RAY

SHOULD SUMMERS IN THE SOUTHERN HEMISPHERE BE WARMER THAN SUMMERS IN THE NORTHERN HEMISPHERE? THE ANSWER IS "YES" AND WINTERS IN THE SOUTHERN HEMISPHERE SHOULD ALSO BE COLDER. IT ALL WILL MAKE SENSE, IF YOU KEEP LOOKING UP!

JOURNEY To A Birthplace of Stars

GREETINGS, **GREETINGS**, FELLOW STARGAZERS! HOW WOULD YOU LIKE TO SEE ONE OF THE TRUE WONDERS OF THE UNIVERSE? WELL, LET ME SHOW YOU!

TO BEGIN WITH, FACE DUE SOUTH—ANY FEBRUARY, ANY YEAR—IN EARLY EVENING.

AND RIGHT IN FRONT OF YOU, YOU WILL SEE THE BRIGHTEST STAR PATTERN OF WINTER: ORION, THE MIGHTY HUNTER.

ORION IS IDENTIFIABLE EVEN TO YOUNG CHILDREN BY HIS THREE EQUALLY SPACED BELT STARS LINED UP IN A ROW, TWO BRIGHT STARS MARKING HIS SHOULDERS, AND TWO BRIGHT STARS MARKING HIS KNEES.

BUT IT'S NOT ANY OF THESE STARS THAT HAPPENS TO BE THE FAVORITE OBJECT OF AMATEURS AROUND THE WORLD. NO, INDEED, IT'S THE MIDDLE STAR OF THE THREE DIM STARS SUSPENDED BELOW ORION'S BELT, POPULARLY CALLED THE SWORD STARS.

IF YOU LOOK CLOSELY AT THE MIDDLE STAR OF THE SWORD, IT LOOKS STRANGE, KIND OF FUZZY. AND NO MATTER HOW HARD YOU TRY TO FOCUS ON IT, IT WON'T APPEAR AS A SHARP, CRISP POINT OF LIGHT.

SQUINT

IN FACT, IF YOU LOOK AT IT WITH A PAIR OF BINOCULARS, IT WILL LOOK SLIGHTLY BIGGER BUT EVEN FUZZIER.

BUT THE STRANGENESS OF THE MIDDLE STAR BECOMES EVEN MORE APPARENT IF WE TAKE A VERY LONG TIME-EXPOSURE PHOTOGRAPH OF IT THROUGH A GOOD AMATEUR TELESCOPE. WHAT DEVELOPS IS TRULY MIND BLOWING...

INDEED, THE MIDDLE SWORD STAR IS NOT A STAR AT ALL, BUT A HUGE NURSERY OF MANY STARS BORN LESS THAN A MILLION YEARS AGO--- WITH MANY MORE COCOONED IN THEIR EMBRYONIC GAS CLOUDS, YET AWAITING BIRTH.

IT'S CALLED THE ORION NEBULA, AND IT IS INCREDIBLY FAR AWAY... 15 HUNDRED LIGHT-YEARS DISTANT. THAT MEANS THAT WHEN WE LOOK AT IT IN OUR CENTURY WE SEE THE LIGHT THAT LEFT IT 15 CENTURIES AGO!

YET THE NEBULA IS SO INCREDIBLY BRIGHT THAT EVEN OUR ANCESTORS NOTED THAT THE MIDDLE STAR IN THE SWORD APPEARED NOT TO BE A STAR AT ALL, BUT SOME STRANGE KIND OF FUZZY LIGHT.

SO SOMETIME IN FEBRUARY, GO OUTSIDE BETWEEN 8 P.M. AND 10 P.M., LOOK DUE SOUTH, AND CONTEMPLATE THIS WONDER OF OF THE UNIVERSE THAT WE IN OUR TIME ARE PRIVILEGED TO BE THE FIRST TO TRULY UNDERSTAND. WOW! WHAT A WONDERFUL TIME TO KEEP LOOKING UP!

A GREAT BIG RED STAR FOR VALENTINE'S DAY

GREETINGS, GREETINGS, FELLOW STARGAZERS! SINCE THE COLOR RED IS ASSOCIATED WITH VALENTINE'S DAY, I THOUGHT I'D TELL YOU ABOUT A SPECIAL COSMIC RED VALENTINE THAT YOU CAN SHARE WITH ALL YOUR LOVED ONES.

IF YOU GO OUT ON ANY VALENTINE'S DAY NIGHT BETWEEN THE HOURS OF 8 AND 9 P.M. AND LOOK DUE SOUTH, YOU'LL SEE A VERY BRIGHT RED STAR SHINING HIGH ABOVE THE HORIZON.

INDEED, IT IS THE BRIGHTEST RED STAR WE CAN SEE WITH THE NAKED EYE FROM PLANET EARTH. IT MARKS THE SHOULDER STAR OF THE GREAT SKY GIANT, ORION, THE HUNTER, AND ITS NAME IS "BETELGEUSE".

IN ARABIC, BETELGEUSE MEANS "THE ARMPIT," WHICH ISN'T VERY ROMANTIC. BUT IF YOU WANT TO GIVE YOUR BELOVED A REALLY BIG VALENTINE, WELL, THIS IS ABOUT AS BIG A ONE AS YOU'LL EVER FIND.

TO REALLY UNDERSTAND THE HUGENESS OF BETELGEUSE, IMAGINE FIRST THAT WE COULD FIT MORE THAN 1 MILLION EARTHS INSIDE OUR SUN. NOW IMAGINE THAT WE COULD FIT OVER 160 MILLION OF OUR SUNS INSIDE OF BETELGEUSE - WHEN IT'S AT ITS SMALLEST SIZE!

1. THE GREAT JACKINI
2. SUN
3. POOF!
4. BETELGEUSE

AND I SAY "SMALLEST SIZE" BECAUSE BETELGEUSE IS ONE OF THOSE STARS THAT CHANGES ITS SIZE REGULARLY, LIKE A HUMONGOUS, SLOWLY PULSATING HEART THAT BEATS ONLY ONCE EVERY SIX YEARS. IF BETELGEUSE WERE OUR SUN, ITS SURFACE WOULD EXTEND TO THE ORBIT OF MARS AT ITS SMALLEST, AND TO THE ORBIT OF JUPITER AT ITS LARGEST. WOW!

SMALLEST SIZE
LARGEST SIZE
SUN
JACK

SO, THERE YOU HAVE IT. A GREAT BIG VALENTINE FOR YOUR SWEETHEART, COURTESY OF OUR LOCAL GALAXY. BUT I STILL RECOMMEND THAT YOU PURCHASE A TRADITIONAL BOX OF CHOCOLATES, WHICH WILL BE FUN TO EAT BY THE LIGHT OF THE VALENTINE'S STAR... IF YOU SIMPLY REMEMBER TO KEEP LOOKING UP!

Harrington

THE BRIGHTEST ST★R IN THE NIGHT SKY

GREETINGS, GREETINGS, FELLOW STAR-GAZERS! OF ALL THE BRIGHT OBJECTS IN THE HEAVENS, ONLY ONE OF THEM HOLDS THE DISTINCTION OF BEING THE BRIGHTEST.

THAT IS, THE BRIGHTEST STAR VISIBLE FROM THE PLANET EARTH, OTHER THAN OUR SUN. LET ME SHOW YOU.

JUST AFTER SUNSET, FACE SOUTHEAST. YOU WILL SEE THE BRIGHTEST CONSTELLATION OF THEM ALL, ORION, THE HUNTER, WITH THREE EQUALLY SPACED STARS IN A ROW MARKING HIS BELT.

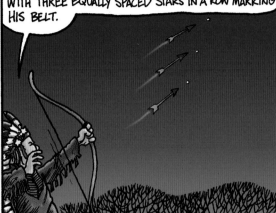

NOW, IF YOU SHOOT AN IMAGINARY ARROW THROUGH ORION'S BELT DOWN TO HIS LEFT, YOU WILL SEE OUR TARGET- THE DAZZLING STAR SIRIUS, WHICH MARKS THE EYE OF ORION'S FAITHFUL COMPANION, CANIS MAJOR, THE GREAT DOG.

YIKES!

PERSONALLY, I PREFER TO CALL SIRIUS BY THE NAME THAT THE ANCIENT EGYPTIANS GAVE IT, THE "SOUL OF ISIS"- A GODDESS OF FERTILITY. BUT WHATEVER NAME IT HAS ENJOYED FOR THE PAST SEVERAL MILLENNIA, IT IS STILL THE BRIGHTEST STAR WE CAN SEE FROM PLANET EARTH.

PAT PAT

BUT THE BRIGHTNESS OF SIRIUS IS ALL AN ILLUSION. IT ONLY APPEARS TO BE THE BRIGHTEST BECAUSE IT IS SO CLOSE TO US, ABOUT 9 LIGHT-YEARS AWAY.

SIRIUS
9 LIGHT-YEARS

WE CAN SEE MANY STARS THAT ARE HUNDREDS OF TIMES LARGER THAN SIRIUS, SUCH AS ORION'S RED SHOULDER STAR, BETELGEUSE. EVEN SO, SIRIUS DOES MAKE OUR OWN STAR, THE SUN, LOOK RATHER PUNY BY COMPARISON, BECAUSE SIRIUS IS ALMOST TWICE AS WIDE.

BETELGEUSE
SIRIUS
SUN

AND IF YOU WATCH SIRIUS WHEN IT IS CLOSE TO THE HORIZON, YOU SHOULD SEE IT FLASH AND SPARKLE AND CHANGE BRILLIANT COLORS- A COSMIC JEWEL UNLIKE ANY OTHER STAR IN THE HEAVENS. IT'S TRULY MAGNIFICENT IF YOU KEEP LOOKING UP!

WALK LIKE AN EGYPTIAN

THE BIRTHDAY STARS of WINTER

GREETINGS, GREETINGS, FELLOW STARGAZERS, WANT TO SEE TWO ABSOLUTELY WONDERFUL STARS THAT CAN BE USED TO CELEBRATE CHILDREN'S BIRTHDAYS? C'MON... I'LL SHOW YOU.

COME THE MIDDLE OF FEBRUARY, JUST STEP OUTSIDE ON ANY CLEAR NIGHT, BETWEEN THE HOURS OF 8 AND 9 P.M., AND LOOK DUE SOUTH. SIRIUS, THE BRIGHTEST STAR IN THE NIGHT SKY, WILL BE RIGHT IN FRONT OF YOU.

SOUTH

SIRIUS MARKS THE EYE OF THE GREAT DOG, CANIS MAJOR. AND IF YOU SHOOT A LINE UP AND TO THE LEFT OF SIRIUS, YOU'LL COME TO PROCYON, WHICH MARKS THE EYE OF THE SMALLER DOG, CANIS MINOR.

PROCYON · CANIS MINOR · SIRIUS · CANIS MAJOR · ROWF!

NOW LET'S COMPARE THE SIZES OF THESE STARS TO OUR SUN.

THE SUN IS 865,000 MILES WIDE... SIRIUS IS 1.4 MILLION MILES WIDE, AND PROCYON IS 1.5 MILLION MILES WIDE.

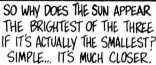

SUN · 865,000 MILES · SIRIUS · 1.4 MILLION MILES · PROCYON · 1.5 MILLION MILES · ARF!

SO WHY DOES THE SUN APPEAR THE BRIGHTEST OF THE THREE IF IT'S ACTUALLY THE SMALLEST? SIMPLE... IT'S MUCH CLOSER.

OUR SUN IS SO CLOSE, IT'S ONLY 93 MILLION MILES AWAY OR 8⅓ LIGHT-MINUTES AWAY. SIRIUS IS 8.6 LIGHT-YEARS FROM EARTH, AND PROCYON IS EVEN FARTHER, 11.4 LIGHT-YEARS AWAY.

CANIS MAJOR · CANIS MINOR · ARF · ARF · RUFF BARK

THUS, PROCYON AND SIRIUS ARE SOMETIMES CALLED THE BIRTHDAY STARS OF 11- AND 9-YEAR OLDS!

WHY? BECAUSE WHEN WE LOOK AT SIRIUS THIS WINTER, WE ARE ACTUALLY SEEING THE LIGHT THAT LEFT IT ABOUT NINE YEARS AGO, WHEN 9-YEAR-OLDS WERE BEING BORN.

CHOMP GULP · HAPPY 9TH

AND THE LIGHT WE SEE FROM PROCYON THIS WINTER ACTUALLY LEFT IT 11 YEARS AGO, WHEN 11-YEAR-OLDS WERE BEING BORN. SO GET YOURSELF OUTSIDE, AND KEEP LOOKING UP!

URP!

CASTOR AND POLLUX ARE THE GEMINI TWINS. IN EARLY EVENING WINTER, THEY FOLLOW ORION ACROSS THE SKY STANDING ON THEIR HEADS.

IF YOU WANT TO SEE THEM UPRIGHT, WAIT UNTIL THE WEE HOURS OF THE MORNING OR UNTIL MAY AFTER SUNSET AND LOOK WEST-NORTHWEST.

I'VE ALWAYS HAD A PROBLEM REMEMBERING WHETHER POLLUX OR CASTOR IS THE BRIGHTER. BUT VERY RECENTLY, I FIGURED OUT AN EASY WAY TO REMEMBER.

POLLUX • • CASTOR

YOU SEE, IN MYTHOLOGY CASTOR WAS A HORSEMAN, WHEREAS POLLUX WAS A BOXER—A PUGILIST. SO WITH THAT IN MIND, I SIMPLY SAY TO MYSELF THAT POLLUX, THE PUGILIST, HAS A LOT MORE PUNCH IN BRIGHTNESS THAN CASTOR. IF YOU CAN REMEMBER THAT, YOU'LL NEVER GET THE TWO OF THEM CONFUSED.

POLLUX, THE PUGILIST, IS 11 TIMES THE DIAMETER OF OUR OWN SUN, AND ALMOST 40 LIGHT-YEARS AWAY.

BUT CASTOR TAKES THE CELESTIAL-WHOPPER PRIZE, BECAUSE IT IS REALLY A MULTIPLE-STAR SYSTEM WITH SIX MEMBERS— ALL SPINNING IN AN INTRICATE COSMIC WALTZ, LIKE THREE STELLAR COUPLES.

BUT NONE OF CASTOR'S STARS IS AS BIG AS POLLUX. PAIR A IS TWICE THE DIAMETER OF OUR SUN, PAIR B IS 1½ TIMES OUR SUN'S DIAMETER. THIS LEAVES C THE ONLY PAIR SMALLER THAN OUR OWN STAR, AND ABOUT ¾ OF OUR SUN'S SIZE. ALL OF THE PAIRS ARE A WHOPPING 50 LIGHT-YEARS AWAY!

SO LOOK EAST FOR THE TWINS, UPSIDE DOWN IN WINTER OR UPRIGHT AFTER SUNSET IN MAY.

CHEATING THE SEASONS

Panel 1: BY NOW, YOU'VE LEARNED THAT THE MOST PROMINENT STARS SEEN EARLY IN THE EVENING ARE CALLED THE STARS OF THE SEASON.

WINTER IS HERE!

Panel 2: EACH SEASON ALSO HAS A CONSTELLATION ASSOCIATED WITH IT— LEO WITH THE SPRING, SCORPIUS WITH SUMMER, PEGASUS WITH AUTUMN, AND ORION WITH WINTER.

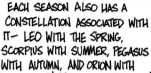

Panel 3: BUT YOU CAN CHEAT THE SEASONS IF YOU PLAY YOUR CARDS RIGHT.

Panel 4: SIMPLY LOOK EAST ABOUT AN HOUR OR TWO BEFORE SUNRISE, AND YOU'LL SEE STAR PATTERNS NOT OF THE CURRENT SEASON, BUT OF AN UPCOMING ONE.

4:00 AM — SUNRISE HILL

Panel 5: FOR INSTANCE, IN SUMMER, SCORPIUS AND SAGITTARIUS ARE IN THE SOUTH BEFORE MIDNIGHT.

SOUTH

YAY!

9:00PM — CLAP CLAP — SUNRISE HILL

Panel 6: BUT IF YOU LOOK EAST AN HOUR OR TWO BEFORE SUNRISE, YOU'LL SEE WINTER'S ORION.

EAST

ALRIGHT, ORION!!

4:00 AM — SUNRISE HILL

Panel 7: JUST REMEMBER THAT IF YOU CAN'T WAIT TO SEE THE STARS OF A DIFFERENT SEASON, DO SOME STARGAZING BEFORE SUNRISE.

YAWN

5:00 AM — YAWN — SUNRISE HILL

Panel 8: AND DID YOU KNOW THAT ORION AND SCORPIUS CAN NEVER BE SEEN IN THE SKY AT THE SAME TIME?

Panel 9: THAT'S BECAUSE, A LONG TIME AGO, ORION GOT STUNG BY THE SCORPION...

OUCH!

Panel 10: ...AND HE'S KEPT A SAFE DISTANCE EVER SINCE. THERE'S SO MUCH TO LEARN ABOUT THE SKY, IF YOU KEEP LOOKING UP!

WHERE'D HE GO?

HARRINGTON

CELESTIAL SCRABBLE

NOW THAT YOU KNOW SOME STARS, I HAVE A GAME FOR YOU TO TRY.

HIDDEN IN THE SKY ARE AN ASSORTMENT OF LETTERS CREATED BY CHANCE ALIGNMENTS OF BRIGHT STARS. YOUR CHALLENGE IS TO TRY TO MAKE WORDS OUT OF THESE LETTERS!

THE MOST FAMOUS LETTER IN THE NIGHT SKY IS THE "W" FORMED BY THE FIVE BRIGHTEST STARS IN THE CONSTELLATION CASSIOPEIA.

BUT IT CAN ALSO APPEAR AS THE LETTER "E" AND THE LETTER "M".

CASSIOPEIA

THERE'S ALSO A LETTER "G" IN THE SKY. IT'S MADE UP OF SEVERAL OF THE MOST BRILLIANT STARS IN THE NIGHT SKY...

LOOK AT THE STAR MAP ON PAGE 80. NOW, TAKE YOUR PENCIL AND CONNECT THE STARS IN THIS **EXACT** ORDER: BETELGEUSE, RIGEL, SIRIUS, PROCYON, POLLUX, CASTOR, CAPELLA, AND FINALLY ALDEBARAN. AND THERE YOU HAVE THE HEAVENLY "G".

CAPELLA
ALDEBARAN
BETELGEUSE
CASTOR
POLLUX
RIGEL
PROCYON
SIRIUS

IF YOU LEAVE OUT BETELGEUSE, AND CONNECT ALDEBARAN AND RIGEL, YOU HAVE A HEXAGONAL "O".

THE FACE OF TAURUS THE BULL IS SHAPED LIKE A "V". TURN THE "V" OVER, CONNECT THE TWO MIDDLE STARS ON EITHER SIDE OF IT, AND YOU HAVE AN "A".

THERE'S EVEN PUNCTUATION MARKS IN THE SKY. THE FAMOUS "SICKLE" OF LEO THE LION LOOKS EXACTLY LIKE A QUESTION MARK...

BUT IT'S BACKWARDS!

AND THERE YOU HAVE IT... SEVEN LETTERS, SOME PUNCTUATION, AND A WORD CHALLENGE.

HOW MANY DID YOU GET?

KEEP LOOKING UP

JACK

ORION'S BELT: FAVORITE STARS WITH NIFTY NAMES

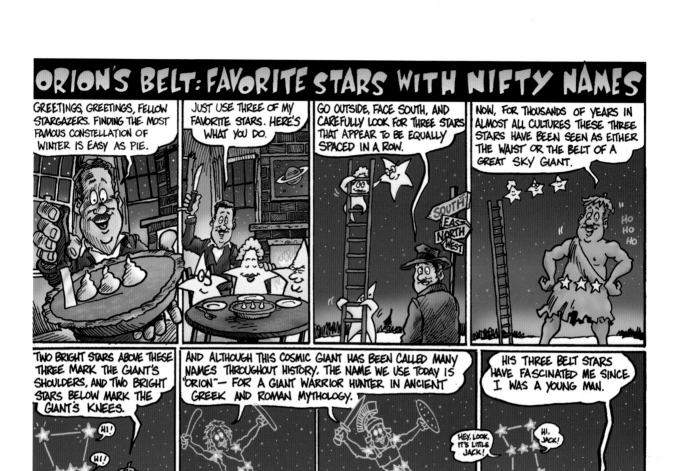

GREETINGS, GREETINGS, FELLOW STARGAZERS. FINDING THE MOST FAMOUS CONSTELLATION OF WINTER IS EASY AS PIE.

JUST USE THREE OF MY FAVORITE STARS. HERE'S WHAT YOU DO.

GO OUTSIDE, FACE SOUTH, AND CAREFULLY LOOK FOR THREE STARS THAT APPEAR TO BE EQUALLY SPACED IN A ROW.

SOUTH EAST NORTH WEST

NOW, FOR THOUSANDS OF YEARS IN ALMOST ALL CULTURES THESE THREE STARS HAVE BEEN SEEN AS EITHER THE WAIST OR THE BELT OF A GREAT SKY GIANT.

HO HO HO

TWO BRIGHT STARS ABOVE THESE THREE MARK THE GIANT'S SHOULDERS, AND TWO BRIGHT STARS BELOW MARK THE GIANT'S KNEES.

HI!

HI!

HI!

AND ALTHOUGH THIS COSMIC GIANT HAS BEEN CALLED MANY NAMES THROUGHOUT HISTORY, THE NAME WE USE TODAY IS "ORION"— FOR A GIANT WARRIOR HUNTER IN ANCIENT GREEK AND ROMAN MYTHOLOGY.

LOOK, THAT'S "OL' PETE."

NO, IT'S "JOLLY."

NO, IT'S "UG"!

LOOK, IT'S ORION THE WARRIOR HUNTER!

HIS THREE BELT STARS HAVE FASCINATED ME SINCE I WAS A YOUNG MAN.

HEY, LOOK, IT'S LITTLE JACK!

HI, JACK!

I JUST LOVE THE SOUND OF THEIR NAMES: ALNILAM, ALNITAK, AND MINTAKA.

ALNILAM ALNITAK MINTAKA

ALNILAM COMES FROM THE ARABIC FOR "STRING OF PEARLS," AND ACTUALLY REFERS TO ALL THREE STARS. ALNITAK MEANS "GIRDLE" AND MINTAKA MEANS "BELT."

BUT NO MATTER WHAT THE NAMES MEAN, I JUST LOVE TO REPEAT THEM—ALNILAM, ALNITAK, AND MINTAKA—BECAUSE THEY SOUND SO POETIC. SAY THEM TO YOURSELF, AS YOU KEEP LOOKING UP!

ALNILAM ALNITAK MINTAKA

HARRINGTON

MORE WAYS TO MEASURE DISTANCES IN THE SKY

GREETINGS, GREETINGS, FELLOW STARGAZERS! YOU PROBABLY KNOW THAT ASTRONOMERS MEASURE DISTANCE BETWEEN CELESTIAL OBJECTS IN DEGREES, BUT DO YOU KNOW HOW BIG 1 DEGREE IS?

I MEAN, HOW MANY OF YOU KNOW HOW TO VISUALIZE JUST HOW BIG 1 DEGREE, OR 5 DEGREES, OR 10 DEGREES REALLY IS?

OK, THE FUNDAMENTAL THING TO REMEMBER IS THAT THE ENTIRE SYSTEM OF MEASURING SKY DISTANCES IS BASED ON THE CIRCLE. WE ALWAYS DIVIDE CIRCLES INTO 360 SECTIONS, OR DEGREES.

SINCE WE CAN ONLY SEE HALF THE SKY AT A TIME, OR HALF A CIRCLE, THE DISTANCE FROM ONE HORIZON TO DIRECTLY OVERHEAD, THE ZENITH, AND BACK DOWN TO THE OPPOSITE HORIZON IS 180 DEGREES.

ZERO DEGREES

180 DEGREES

WHICH ALSO MEANS THAT THE DISTANCE FROM ANY POINT ON THE HORIZON TO DIRECTLY OVERHEAD, THE ZENITH, IS 90 DEGREES, SO, OF COURSE, THE DISTANCE FROM A CLEAR FLAT HORIZON TO HALFWAY UP TO THE ZENITH WILL BE HALF OF 90 DEGREES, OR 45 DEGREES, AND SO ON.

90 DEGREES "THE ZENITH"

45 DEGREES

BUT THERE'S AN EVEN BETTER WAY TO VISUALIZE 1 DEGREE. THE FULL MOON IS ½ A DEGREE WIDE, SO 1 DEGREE IS 2 FULL MOONS WIDE.

1 DEGREE

NOW, HERE'S A WONDERFUL TRICK YOU CAN USE IN CASE THE MOON'S NOT OUT. SIMPLY USE YOUR HAND OUTSTRETCHED AT ARM'S LENGTH, YOUR PINKY FINGER WILL MEASURE 1 DEGREE AGAINST THE SKY, 3 FINGERS WILL MEASURE 5 DEGREES, AND YOUR FIST, 10 DEGREES.

1 DEGREE

5 DEGREES

10 DEGREES

THE DISTANCE BETWEEN YOUR PINKY FINGER AND YOUR INDEX FINGER, STRETCHED OUT, IS 15 DEGREES. SO, IF YOU EVER WANT TO CHECK OUT HOW HIGH THE SUN OR MOON IS ABOVE THE HORIZON, JUST STRETCH OUT YOUR ARM AND LET YOUR FINGERS DO THE MEASURING. IT'S EASY IF YOU KEEP LOOKING UP!

MANY OF THE BRIGHTEST STARS AND PLANETS CAN BE SEEN FROM URBAN AREAS, BUT YOU'LL SEE MUCH MORE IF YOU GET AWAY FROM CITY LIGHTS.

TO SEE THE MILKY WAY BEST, YOU ALSO NEED A NIGHT WITHOUT A BRIGHT MOON.

S'LONG, FELLOWS!

WITH THE NAKED EYE YOU CAN SEE 2,000 TO 3,000 STARS ON A DARK MOONLESS NIGHT. BUT BINOCULARS OR A SMALL TELESCOPE WILL REVEAL THOUSANDS MORE!

BINOCULARS ARE GREAT FOR LOOKING AT OUR MOON, JUPITER'S MOONS, STAR CLUSTERS, GASEOUS NEBULAE, AND DISTANT GALAXIES.

AND MANY TELESCOPES NOW HAVE BUILT-IN COMPUTERS THAT WILL FIND THESE OBJECTS FOR YOU.

FIND THE PLEIADES!

WHAT... AGAIN?

BEFORE YOU BUY ANY STARGAZING EQUIPMENT, BE SURE TO LOOK THROUGH A FRIEND'S BINOCULARS AND TELESCOPE FIRST. ALSO CONSIDER JOINING AN ASTRONOMY CLUB, WHERE YOU CAN STARGAZE WITH NEW FRIENDS.

STAR PARTY TONITE!

STAR CHART

BUT FIRST AND FOREMOST, LEARN TO IDENTIFY AS MANY CONSTELLATIONS AS YOU CAN.

HEH HEH

THERE'S ORION... CANIS MAJOR...

STAR WHEEL

IF YOU SEE AN UNFAMILIAR STAR IN A CONSTELLATION, CHANCES ARE YOU'VE SPOTTED A PLANET.

HEY! I'VE FOUND A NEW STAR! WOO HOO!

NO, THAT'S VENUS

STAR WHEEL

IS IT TWINKLING? STARS "TWINKLE" WHILE PLANETS DO NOT!

ROCK STEADY!

HARRINGTON

FUN ASTRO FACTS

SPRING STAR MAP

REMEMBER, IF YOU SEE A BRIGHT STAR IN A CONSTELLATION THAT ISN'T NORMALLY THERE, YOU'VE PROBABLY SPOTTED A PLANET. PLANETS CONSTANTLY CHANGE THEIR POSITIONS AMONG THE STARS FROM NIGHT TO NIGHT. CAN YOU FIND THE BRIGHT "BEEHIVE" STAR CLUSTER (M44) IN CANCER, THE CRAB? LOOK FIRST WITH YOUR NAKED EYE, THEN WITH BINOCULARS.

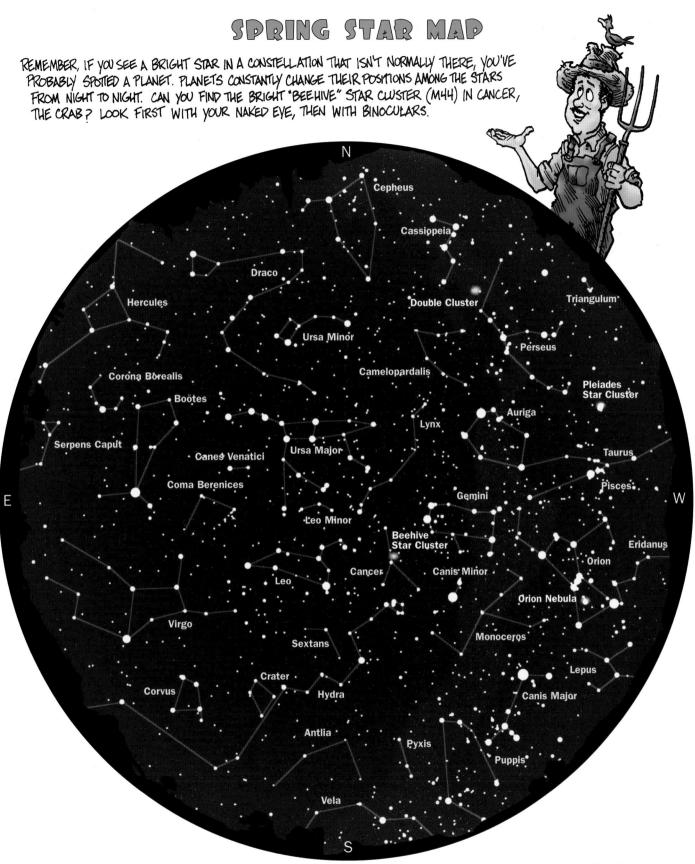

The monthly All-Sky Chart depicts the sky (minus the moon and planets) as it appears in late March around 1:00 a.m., mid-April around 11:00 p.m., and mid-May around 9:00 p.m.

SUMMER STAR MAP

REMEMBER, STARS "TWINKLE" BUT PLANETS DO NOT. USE BINOCULARS TO LOOK FOR TWO BRIGHT STAR CLUSTERS (M6 AND M7) NEAR THE TAIL OF SCORPIUS, THE SCORPION. DID YOU NOTICE HOW RED ANTARES LOOKS?

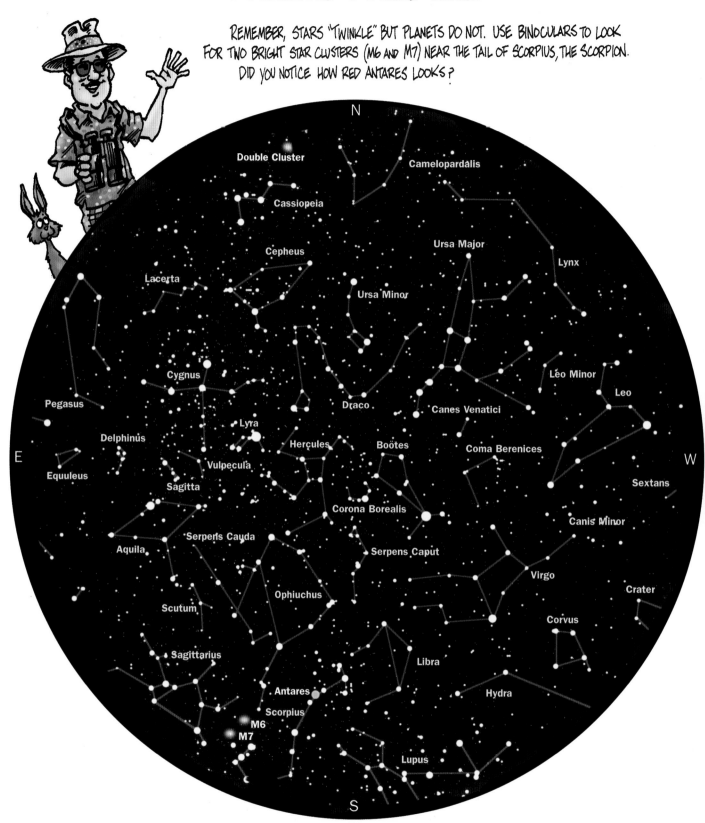

The monthly All-Sky Chart depicts the sky (minus the moon and planets) as it appears in late June around midnight, late July around 10:00 p.m., and early August around 9:00 p.m.

AUTUMN STAR MAP

REMEMBER, ONLY THE BRIGHTEST STARS AND PLANETS CAN BE SEEN FROM URBAN AREAS. YOU'LL SEE MUCH MORE IF YOU OBSERVE AWAY FROM CITY LIGHTS. THE GREAT ANDROMEDA GALAXY IS A NAKED-EYE OBJECT FROM A DARK-SKY SITE. IT LOOKS EVEN BETTER THROUGH BINOCULARS! THE FAMOUS DOUBLE CLUSTER IN PERSEUS — TWO STAR CLUSTERS SIDE BY SIDE — IS BEAUTIFUL THROUGH BINOCULARS AND SPECTACULAR IN A TELESCOPE!!

N

Lynx

Ursa Major

Auriga

Camelopardalis

Draco

Boötes

Ursa Minor

Corona Borealis

Taurus

Perseus

Cepheus

Double Cluster

Cassiopeia

Hercules

Serpens Caput

Pleiades Star Cluster

Triangulum

Andromeda

Cygnus

Lyra

Aries

Andromeda Galaxy

Lacerta

Vulpecula

Ophiuchus

Pegasus

Sagitta

Aquila

Delphinus

Scutum

Serpens Cauda

Cetus

Pisces

Equuleus

Aquarius

Sagittarius

Capricornus

Sculptor

Piscis Austrinus

Microscopium

Grus

S

E

W

The monthly All-Sky Chart depicts the sky (minus the moon and planets) as it appears mid-September around 10:00 p.m., mid-October around 8:00 p.m., and mid-November around 6:00 p.m.

WINTER STAR MAP

REMEMBER, THIS IS A GOOD MONTH TO PLAY CELESTIAL SCRABBLE! THE PLEIADES STAR CLUSTER, ALSO KNOWN AS THE SEVEN SISTERS, IS FREQUENTLY MISTAKEN FOR THE LITTLE DIPPER. ONE OF THE MOST GLORIOUS OBJECTS IN THE HEAVENS, THE GREAT ORION NEBULA (M42), CAN BE SEEN WITH THE NAKED EYE IN ORION'S SWORD. BE SURE TO LOOK AT IT THROUGH BINOCULARS!

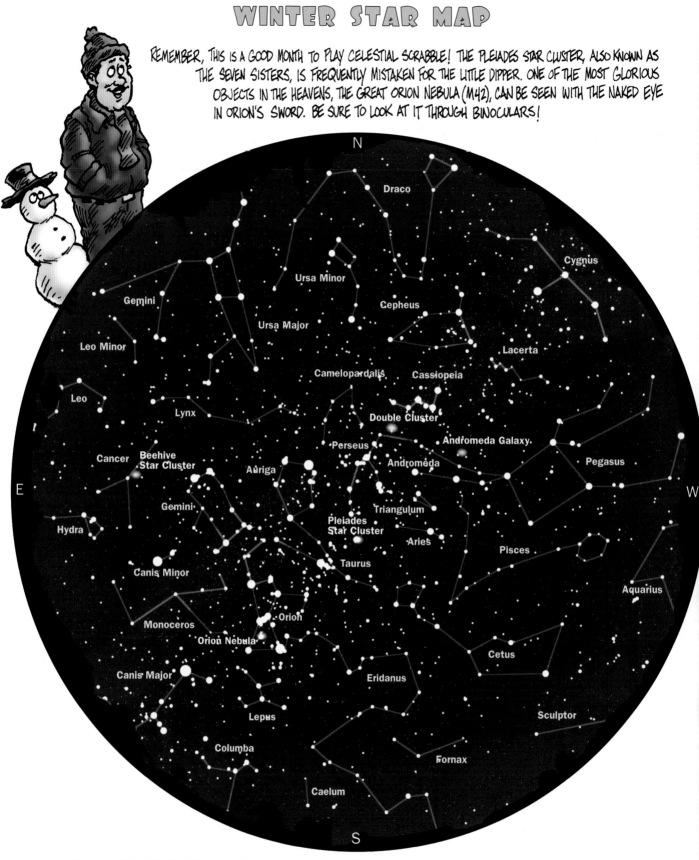

The monthly All-Sky Chart depicts the sky (minus the moon and planets) as it appears mid-December around 10:00 p.m., mid-January around 8:00 p.m., and mid-February around 6:00 p.m.

GLOSSARY

"Apex of the Sun's way" — The point in the night sky toward which the Sun and the solar system are moving. This point is in the constellation Hercules but close to the star Vega in Lyra.

Asterism — A distinctive pattern of stars, such as the Big Dipper or Summer Triangle, that forms part of one or more constellations.

Axis — An imaginary straight line about which a body turns or about which a system (like the night sky) appears to rotate.

Celestial sphere — The imaginary sphere surrounding the Earth, with the stars and the other astronomical objects appearing to be attached to it.

Comet — A minor celestial body resembling a "dirty snowball," between 0.1 and 100 miles across, that travels around the Sun, usually in an elliptical orbit. A comet has a fuzzy coma and often grows a tail that gets longer as it nears the Sun.

Constellation — One of the 88 parts into which the sky is divided; also refers to the historical, mythological, or other figures that represent earlier divisions of the sky.

Degree — The unit astronomers use to measure the distance between the stars as seen from the Earth.

Earthshine — Sunlight reflected off the Earth, which dimly lights the side of the Moon that does not receive direct light from the Sun.

Ecliptic — The plane of the Earth's orbit projected onto the sky. Also the apparent path of the Sun and planets among the stars.

Ellipse — A closed curve (elliptical orbit) that describes the orbits of bodies in space.

Equinox — Either of two times during a year (vernal equinox and autumnal equinox) when the Sun crosses the celestial equator and the length of day and night are approximately equal.

"False dawn" — (see Zodiacal Light)

Galaxy — A giant collection of stars, gas, and dust held together by gravity. Our galaxy, the Milky Way, contains about 100 billion stars.

Horizon — The apparent intersection of the Earth and sky as seen by an observer.

Indian summer — A period of mild weather occurring in late autumn or early winter.

Interstellar — Between the stars.

Kepler's Laws of Motion — Three fundamental laws of planetary motion. The laws were first worked out by Johannes Kepler between 1609 and 1619. Law 1 describes the elliptical shape of planetary orbits; Law 2 describes the speed at which the planets travel in their orbits; and Law 3 describes the length of time a planet takes to orbit the Sun.

Light pollution — Excess artificial light, mainly from cities, that illuminates the night sky and obscures the stars.

Light-year — The distance that light travels in a vacuum in one year, about 6 trillion miles.

Meridian — A great circle passing through the two poles of the celestial sphere and the zenith of a given observer. (See Zenith)

Meteor — (also called "falling star" or "shooting star") A bright trail or streak that appears in the sky when a meteoroid is heated to glowing by friction with the Earth's atmosphere.

Meteoroid — A solid body moving in space that is smaller than an asteroid and at least as large as a speck of dust.

Meteor shower — The appearance of many meteors with approximately parallel paths during a short period of time, as the Earth passes through a comet's orbit. Major meteor showers are named for the constellation from which they appear to radiate.

Nebula — Interstellar regions of gas and dust.

Orbit — The path followed by one body around another body in space that is influenced by gravity. Also, one complete revolution of such a body around another.

Perspective — The appearance of objects in depth as perceived by normal binocular vision.

Radiant — The location on the celestial sphere from which meteors in a shower appear to burst forth because of perspective.

Solstice — Either of two times of the year when the Sun is at its greatest distance from the celestial equator. The summer solstice in the Northern Hemisphere occurs about June 21, and the winter solstice in the same hemisphere occurs about December 21.

Zenith — The point on the celestial sphere that is directly above the observer.

Zodiac — The collection of 12 constellations (beginning with Aries, the Ram, and ending with Pisces, the Fishes) through which the Sun appears to travel throughout the course of one year.

Zodiacal light — A faint light seen along the ecliptic and possibly due to sunlight being scattered by interplanetary dust. It is seen for a few hours after sunset or for a few hours before sunrise, which is why it is also called the "false dawn."

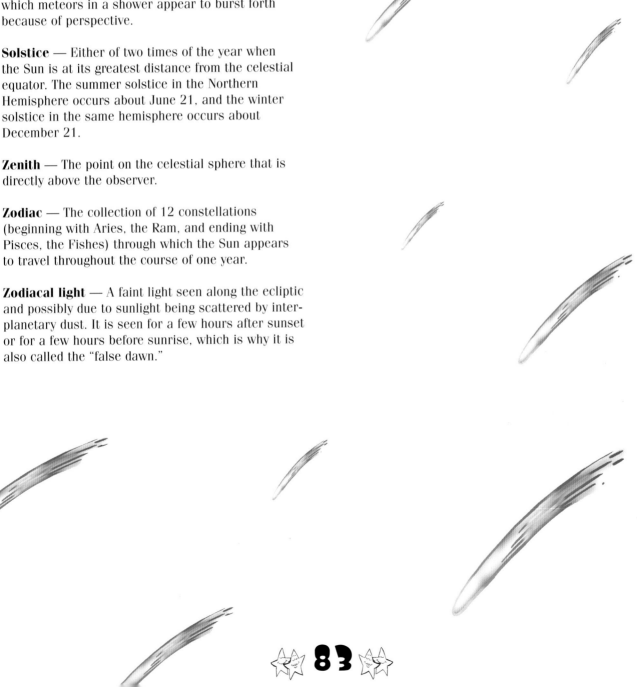

INDEX

Alcor: 32

Aldebaran: 32

Alpha Centauri: 51, 73

Altair: 38, 39, 52

Amphitrite: 40

Ancient Egypt: 9

Antares: 41

Andromeda:
   constellation: 51
   galaxy: 51, 79

"apex of the Sun's way": 46

Aquila, the Eagle: 38, 47, 52

Arcturus: 37

Aries, the Ram (also Lamb): 35

Autumn Square: 47

Beehive Cluster: 77

Betelgeuse: 58, 62, 67

Big Bear: *See* Big Dipper

Big Dog: *See* Canis Major

Big Dipper: 30, 31, 32, 37

"Birthday Stars": 64

"Bragging Stars": 50

Caesar, Julius: 41

Canis Major: 58, 63, 64

Canis Minor: 58, 64

Capella: 67

Cassiopeia: 48, 50, 51, 67

Castor: 65, 67

comets: 42

constellations: 77–80

Cygnus, the Swan: 47, 52

Delphinus, the Dolphin: 40

Deneb: 36, 38, 39, 47, 52

Denebola: 36

distances, measuring sky: 6, 16, 21, 22, 26, 28, 31,
   42, 51, 70, 73

Dubhe: 31

earthshine: 8

ellipse: 56, 59

equinox: (autumnal) 11, 44; (vernal) 34, 44, 55

"false dawn": 45

Galilei, Galileo: 20

Geminids (Geminid meteor shower): 53

Gemini, the Twins: 65

Great Square: *See* Pegasus

Herschel, Sir William: 22

Indian summer: 46

"Job's Coffin": 40

Khayyam, Omar: 45

Kepler's Laws of Motion: 56

Leo, the Lion: 33, 35, 36, 66, 67
   "Sickle": 67

Leonids (Leonid meteor shower): 53

Lesath: 42

Libra: 41, 43

light pollution: 50

light-years: 26, 36, 37, 39, 42, 43, 51, 61, 63, 64, 65

Little Bear: *See* Little Dipper

Little Dipper: 30, 80

Lyra, the Lyre (Harp): 38, 46, 47, 52

M6 (cluster): 42, 78

M7 (cluster): 42, 78

maria: 12

Maya: 72

Merak: 31

meridian: 57

meteor (shower): 53, 54

Milky Way (galaxy): 43, 48, 50, 71

Mizar: 32

Moon:
   blue: 13
   cat goddess: 9
   crescent: 6, 7, 8
   gibbous: 7
   harvest: 11
   lady in the: 12
   man in the: 12
   new: 7
   optical illusion: 10
   phases of: 7, 18
   size of: 6

"New Year's Eve Star": 57

North Star: *See* Polaris

Orion, the Hunter: 33, 58, 60, 62, 66, 68
   nebula: 61, 80

Pegasus: 51, 66

perspective: 54

planets:
   disguised as stars: 17
   Jupiter: 19, 20, 21, 23
     Great Red Spot: 20
     King of Planets: 21
     moons of (Io, Europa, Ganymede, Callisto): 20
   Mars: 19, 22, 41
     Valles Marineris: 19
   Mercury: 18
   Neptune: 23

order of: 14, 15
  Pluto: 23, 56
    Charon: 23
   Saturn: 21, 23
  Uranus ("George"): 22, 23
  Venus ("morning star"): 18
Pleiades (star cluster): 49, 80
Polaris: 26, 27, 29, 30, 50, 51
Pollux: 65, 67
Poseidon: 40
Procyon: 58, 64, 67
Proxima Centauri: 26
radiant: 54
Regulus: 36
Rigel: 67
Sagittarius, the Archer: 43, 48, 66
Scorpius, the Scorpion: 41, 42, 43, 48, 66, 78
seasons: 28, 34, 35
"Seven Sisters": 49, 80
Shaula: 42
Sirius: 57, 58, 63, 64, 67
Small Dog: *See* Canis Minor
solstice: (winter) 55, 56; (summer) 55
"Soul of Isis": 63
Spica: 37
"Spring of the Year": 34
Stars:
  changing position of: 27, 28
  measuring the distance of: 26
  of the season: 47, 66
  what they are: 25
Summer Triangle: 38–39, 46, 47, 48, 52
Sun:
  Earth closest to: 56
  eclipse of: 16
  light from: 25
  size of: 16
"Sword Stars": 60
Taurus, the Bull: 67
Teapot: 43
Tennyson, Lord: 49
Tombaugh, Clyde: 23
Urakhga: 52
"Valentine Star": *See* Betelgeuse
Vega: 38, 39, 46, 47
Winter Triangle: 58
Zenith: 38, 48, 70
Zodiac: 45
"zodiacal light": 45

Jack Horkheimer is executive director of the Miami Space Transit Planetarium and creator, writer, and host of public television's *Star Gazer*, a weekly series on naked-eye astronomy. *Star Gazer* celebrates its 30th anniversary in November 2006.

Jack appears frequently on major TV and radio network talk shows and has narrated several solar eclipses for CNN. In his passion to bring astronomy to the public, he has led several solar eclipse expeditions and organized the first supersonic Halley's Comet Chase aboard Concorde jets.

Over his long career Jack has received numerous awards, including the Astronomical Society of the Pacific's Klumpke-Roberts Award for popularizing astronomy and the Astronomical League's prestigious Outstanding Achievement Award. The International Astronomical Union named asteroid 11409 Horkheimer in his honor. He is a founding member of the International Planetarium Society, founding co-editor of *The Planetarian*, and a past editor of *Southern Skies*.

Jack enjoys his cartoon alter ego and was delighted recently to be the summer weekend host on Time/Warner's Cartoon Network. Recognized worldwide for his TV sign-off, "Keep Looking Up," he has already chosen his epitaph: "Keep Looking Up was my life's admonition. I can do little else in my present position." Until then, he plans to remain vertical well into the third millennium at his home in Pinecrest, Florida.

Star Gazer can be downloaded over the Internet at www.jackstargazer.com. The Star Gazer Web site is a Key Resource Award winner.

Stephen James O'Meara is a contributing editor for *ODYSSEY* magazine and is *Sky & Telescope* magazine's "Eye on the Sky" columnist. He is the recipient of numerous awards, including the prestigious Lone Stargazer Award for his pre-Voyager visual discovery of the spokes in Saturn's B-ring and for being the first to determine visually the rotation period of Uranus. He has authored or co-authored seven books. The International Astronomical Union named asteroid 3637 O'Meara in his honor. A graduate of Northeastern University, O'Meara is also a National Geographic–funded explorer and contract photographer/videographer specializing in volcanic eruptions. He lives with his wife, Donna, in Volcano, Hawaii.

Rich Harrington is an award-winning freelance illustrator whose work has appeared in books, magazines, and newspapers. He is an assistant professor in the Illustration Department at Moore College of Art and Design in Philadelphia. A graduate of Syracuse University, he is a member of the Society of Illustrators and the Philadelphia Sketch Club. He lives with his wife and two daughters in Newtown, Pennsylvania. Over his eight years drawing the "Stargazing with Jack Horkheimer" cartoon for *ODYSSEY* magazine, Harrington says that he has, indeed, done a lot of looking up.

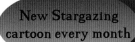